Dedicated to

Sigurd Olson,
Michael Frome
and the late
Freeman Tilden,

whose love for
America's national parks
and the words that
sprang from their hearts
have been an
inspiration.

CLB 2034
© 1988 Colour Library Books Ltd., Guildford, Surrey, England.
All right reserved.
Printed and bound in Barcelona, Spain by Cronion, S.A.
1988 edition published by Crescent Books, distributed by Crown Publishers, Inc.
ISBN 0 517 64946 2
h g f e d c b a

ALASKA

Fairbanks

Mount
McKinley
NP

Anchorage

GULF OF ALASKA

Olympic
NP

North
Cascades NP

WASHINGTON

Mount Rainier NP

Portland

PACIFIC NORTHWEST

OREGON

Crater Lake NP

Boise

IDAHO

CANADA

Glacier NP

Fort Benton

MONTANA

Billings

Yellowstone NP

Grand Teton NP

WYOMING

ROCKY MOUNTAIN

Redwood NP

Lassen
Volcanic NP

Sacramento

San
Francisco

NEVADA

WESTERN

Yosemite NP

Kings Canyon NP

Sequoia NP

Las
Vegas

CALIFORNIA

Los Angeles

Channel
Islands NP

San Diego

Salt Lake City

UTAH

Capitol
Reef NP

Zion NP

Bryce Canyon NP

Grand Canyon NP

ARIZONA

Phoenix

Rocky M

Denver

COLORADO

Arches NP

Canyonlands NP

Mesa Verde NP

Santa Fe

Albuquerque

NEW MEXICO

Petrified
Forest NP

Carlsbad
Caverns NP

El Paso

Guadalup
Mountains

Big Bend

MEXICO

OAHU

MOLOKAI

Honolulu

MAUI

Haleakala
NP

HAWAII

PACIFIC OCEAN

WESTERN

Hawaii
Volcanoes NP

ATLANTIC OCEAN

Virgin
Islands NP

San Juan

PUERTO
RICO

SOUTHEAST

NATIONAL PARK SERVICE U.S. DEPARTMENT OF THE INTERIOR, Regional offices:-

ALASKA
540 West 5th Avenue
Room 202
Anchorage, AK 99501

PACIFIC NORTHWEST
601 4th and Pike Bldg.
Seattle, WA 98101
Phone: (206) 442-0170

MIDWEST
1709 Jackson Street
Omaha, NE 68102
Phone: (402) 221-3471

MID-ATLANTIC
143 South Third Street
Philadelphia, PA 19106
Phone: (215) 597-7018

NORTH ATLANTIC
15 State Street
Boston, MA 02109
Phone: (617) 223-0058

WESTERN
450 Golden Gate Avenue
P.O. Box 36063
San Francisco, CA 94102
Phone: (415) 556-4122

ROCKY MOUNTAIN
P.O. Box 25287
Denver, CO 80225
Phone: (303) 234-3095

SOUTHWEST
P.O. Box 728
Santa Fe, NM 87501
Phone: (505) 988-6375

SOUTHEAST
Richard B. Russell, Federal
Bldg. & U.S. Courthouse
75 Spring Street, S.W.
Atlanta, GA 30303
Phone: (404) 221-5187

NATIONAL CAPITAL
1100 Ohio Drive, S.W.
Washington, DC 20242
Phone: (202) 426-6700

Featuring the Photography of:
William Curwen, Eberhard Streichan,
Nick Meers, Edmund Nagële FRPS,
Neil Sutherland, Peter Beney.

NATIONAL PARKS OF THE U.S.A.

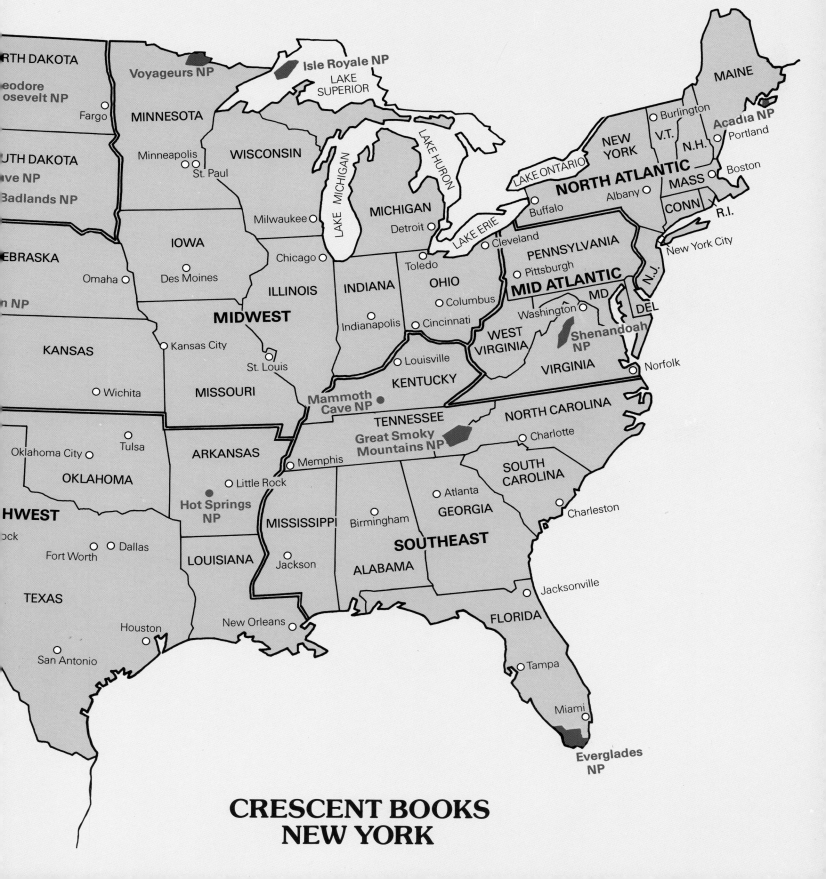

CRESCENT BOOKS
NEW YORK

INTRODUCTION

As the final words of this manuscript are being written, Mount St. Helens in the State of Washington is erupting. "The gods are angry in the Cascades," the *New York Times* headlined. Indeed, it has been an awesome experience. To a nation that annually loses lives and property in staggering figures, the power of St. Helens has been mind-shattering. And the best predictions are that it could be years before the volcano finally rests.

This is the first volcanic eruption in the continental United States since Mount Lassen, 400 miles to the south in California, exploded in 1914 and 1915. Probably no worse in its destruction than Lassen, Mount St. Helens has been a media event, to put it in electronic-age parlance. Virtually every rumble of the earth, every belch of steam and ash, has been reported to the world, sometimes within minutes of its happening. No other volcano in history has received such global attention. And yet somewhere between the tragic loss of precious lives and valuable timberlands and the selling of souvenir ash for a dollar on the streets of Seattle, the real significance of what has taken place has been overshadowed.

Mount St. Helens has told us – perhaps reminded us is better – tragically, yet so vividly, that all is not yet done on this earth. The Colorado River slowly grinds away at the floor of the Grand Canyon, and at Bryce and Zion and Arches and the Canyonlands of Utah, the winds and rains inexorably carve and slice the landscape, but here the processes are exceedingly slow and these places have become attractions of beauty where changes are barely perceived from one generation to the next. But suddenly on Sunday, May 18, 1980, in one mighty burst of nature that, according to experts, equaled 500 times the force of the atomic bomb dropped on Hiroshima, the earth moved and within hours had significantly altered more than 150 square miles of the planet and affected thousands more beyond.

It was not exactly without warning that St. Helens blew. The last recorded series of eruptions began in 1831 and lasted for twenty-five years, all when the land was sparsely populated and communications to the outside world non-existent. And then all was quiet. But in 1978, just two years in advance, two U.S. Geological Survey volcanologists wrote: "In the future, Mount St. Helens probably will erupt violently and intermittently just as it has in the recent geologic past, and these future eruptions will affect human life and health, property, agriculture and general economic welfare over a broad area."

When you stand by a Giant Sequoia or at the rim of the Grand Canyon or at the base of the Rocky Mountains, it is for but a second on the great calendar of time, and one thinks that here time has stopped, that the trees, the rivers, the mountains have always been like this and they always will be. It's difficult to envision the natural processes that created these things, the processes that are still going on. There has been little change in the Grand Canyon since John Wesley Powell first explored the Colorado; the big trees still grow yet they have not significantly altered in appearance since first discovered; and the mountains move beneath the surface without much to jar our security.

But John Muir, standing atop the California Sierras, understood. "The last days of this glacial winter are not yet past, so young is our world," he wrote. "I used to envy the father of our race, dwelling as he did in contact with the new-made fields and plants of Eden; but I do so no more, because I have discovered that I also live in creation's dawn; the morning stars still sing together, and the world, not yet half-made, becomes more beautiful every day."

Mount St. Helens is but the latest manifestation of "creation's dawn"; and "a world not yet half-made." It goes on right before our eyes. Recently, following scenes of the Grand Canyon, a television commentator graphically remarked: "And if you don't fix that leak in the outside faucet, that's what your backyard will look like in a couple of million years."

Mount St. Helens is not a national park, although it may be someday. Within a few weeks following the first eruption there was talk among the powers in Washington that the U.S. Forest Service, under whose domain the mountain and its timberland had been administered, would offer it to the National Park Service. Even President Carter, following his visit to the disaster area, hinted at new economic possibilities in the volcano and its environs. "People will come from all over the world to observe the impressiveness of the force of nature. . . . it would be, . . . a tourist attraction that would equal the Grand Canyon."

The President's words did little to encourage the devastated people of the Northwest, and no doubt National Park Service officials cringed at the mammoth responsibilities of administering, protecting, and interpreting the volcano as a National Park. Yet this could be. This is what the National Park Service is all about, and if such is the mandate of the United States Congress, Mount St. Helens will pass into the hands of the best and most experienced organization in the world to preserve this geologic phenomenon for the future.

Without doubt controversy will rage over St. Helens – preservation for its scientific importance and/or for the "pleasure" of the people. Exponents of both will be at loggerheads, one arguing that the mountain cannot be trampled by anyone but scientists, the other saying the public must have an opportunity to see, experience, enjoy. The fact is that both will win out in the end, for this too is what national parks are all about.

John Muir wrote in 1898: "Thousands of nerve-shaken, overcivilized people are beginning to find out that going to the mountains is going home; that wilderness is a necessity; and that mountain parks and reservations are useful not only as fountains of timber and irrigating rivers, but as fountains of life." Muir was talking about the Yosemites and Sequoias and Yellowstones, but were he alive today, without question he .would support the preservation of Mount St. Helens as a "fountain of knowledge."

There are 322 areas in the National Park Service, a total of some seventy-six million acres of the United States set aside for the public. Forty of these areas are designated National Parks; all but one, Mesa Verde, representing the most significant natural features of the North American continent. These are, in the truest sense, America's national treasures; perhaps more importantly they are treasures belonging to the world, a modern-day calendar upon which we measure the earth, our tenancy on it, and, if we perceive it correctly, the future. Virtually every acre of the forty parks, including Mesa Verde, is inexorably linked to the passage of time and the fragile, unsure thread of tomorrow.

The spectacles of Acadia, the Everglades, Mount McKinley, the Badlands . . . they all belie the turmoil which orchestrated their beginnings as national parks. In fact, one must marvel that they exist at all. But for a handful of farsighted individuals, names most Americans would not readily recognize, we would not see, let alone ever really understand, how this land was formed, how it appeared in its original state, the role nature has played in our lives. These were men of vision who saw and held fast to their convictions, and, ultimately, set a course of preservation that would extend to the far reaches of the globe.

That America pioneered the national park idea is true. That it all began solely as an effort to preserve the country's natural beauty and resources is doubtful, and we live under no illusions. But after more than a century of national parks, the early motives are immaterial. It makes little difference how they began. The treasures are ours and it will forever be a mark on mankind how they are preserved. A national park is a "fountain of life," said John Muir. Enos Mills, the "father of Rocky Mountain National Park," added: "Without parks and outdoor life all that is best in civilization will be smothered. To save ourselves – to enable us to live at our best and happiest, parks are necessary. Within national parks there is room – glorious room – room in which to find ourselves, in which to think and hope, to dream and plan, to rest and resolve."

"There is nothing more practical than the preservation of beauty, than the preservation of anything that appeals to the higher emotions of mankind," said President Theodore Roosevelt. The following essays do nothing more than that – appeal to the higher emotions of mankind. There is no crusade for conservation or preservation; that is done by writers far more experienced. Influenced by those writers? Yes! But the theme set forth here is merely an appreciation of the beauty Teddy Roosevelt talked about.

America's national parks are a part of our lives, perhaps even a symbol of our very existence. Disrespect, disregard, destruction . . . a view through visionless eyes . . . this could forecast our fate with far more truth than the political intrigues of despots.

Elder Zosima, a character in Fyodor Dostoevsky's *The Brothers Karamazov,* said it all:

Brothers, . . . Love God's creation, love every atom of it separately, and love it also as a whole; love every green leaf, every ray of God's light; love the animals and the plants and love every inanimate object. If you come to love all things, you will perceive God's mystery inherent in all things; once you have perceived it, you will understand it better and better every day. And finally you will love the whole world with a total universal love.

James V. Murfin
Rockville, Maryland
1980

Snow is shoveled from an ice fishing house on a sub-zero morning at Cranberry Bay, Rainy Lake right, *eloquently emphasizing that winter in Voyageurs National Park is a force to be reckoned with.* (Photo: Fred Hirschmann).

Voyageurs National Park

Be it enacted by the Senate and House of Representatives of the United States of America in Congress Assembled: That the purpose of this Act is to preserve, for the inspiration and enjoyment of present and future generations, the outstanding scenery, geological conditions and waterway systems which constituted a part of the Voyageurs who contributed to the opening of the Northwestern United States.
Public Law 91-662, January 8, 1971

The histories of Rocky Mountain, Grand Teton, and Yellowstone National Parks hint at the fur trade of the eighteenth and early nineteenth centuries that brought a unique breed of man into this vast wilderness looking for the beaver and sent him home filled with tales of wonder. Their stories are more often than not shadowed by what they found – the mountains, rivers, glaciers, and other geological phenomena that, in most cases, were merely barriers.

Here is a national park, however, that not only encompasses within its boundaries some of the very land where trappers plied their trade, but honors the profession by name: Voyageurs National Park.

It is, of course, much more than a monument to an important chapter of American history, for the things associated with these extraordinary frontiersmen – the forts and trails – have long since vanished. But the lakes and forests they traveled have been little disturbed and here in Northern Minnesota, just east of International Falls and along the Canadian border, are 219,000 acres of pristine North Woods – fir, spruce, pine, aspen, and birch – as they saw them.

Surely men explored North America because that was the nature of the pioneers who, no sooner landing on the Eastern shores, moved toward the West in search of land and food. Timber, gold, and a dozen other attractions drew them, acre by acre, mile by mile, into the frontiers. But the North American beaver, probably more than any other single factor in those early days, was responsible for the gradual exploration of the North Country.

Back in Europe, where the whims of fashion had already changed the course of history many times, one more, the beaver hat, set in motion the conquering of a land, wars between nations, and the beginning of an industry that still thrives. A beaver hat was a prized possession in the 1600's, a sign of wealth and high social status. But the European beaver was small and its fur was no match for the large pelts found in North America. The first traders, who explored what is now Minnesota, returned to England in 1666 with furs worth $100,000. They had found America's first gold, and for the next 200 years they mined it methodically and with a passion.

First there was the trader or the trading company – and trading it was, for there were no cash transactions on this side of the Atlantic. The trader bought items in

Europe – knives, mirrors, pots, needles, wine – that were negotiable with the trappers. The trapper furnished the beaver pelts in exchange. Now we come to the voyageur. He was the middleman, so to speak. The voyageur carried the merchandise to the trading posts in the wilderness and returned with the furs. Today this is a simple matter, but it took a special kind of human being in the eighteenth and nineteenth centuries to be a voyageur, and that's what this park is all about.

At first the Indians came to the trader – trade fairs at Montreal and Quebec. As competition increased and hostilities grew between tribes, and the "beaver frontier" pushed back, the trader began intercepting the trapper in the wilds. Soon the pattern reversed, and the trader was going virtually to the traps himself.

Voyageur is French for "traveler," a man who could survive the most strenuous journeys through the uncharted forests, streams and rivers of the North Country, paddling canoes, carrying supplies, and coping with rigorous weather conditions. He was French-Canadian, short (about five feet, six inches), rugged, and a member of what became a very elite society. There were two voyageurs: those who traveled west with the merchandise, and those who lived in the wilderness and dealt with the Indians and then trekked from the Northwest trapping outposts eastward. They met at Grand Portage on the shores of Lake Superior.

What made these people so special was their inordinate strength and endurance. They traveled thousands of miles by canoe, some thirty-five feet long, with a crew of twelve, and carried their cargoes hundreds of miles over land at portages. A trip west from Montreal began as soon as the river ice melted and ended at Grand Portage in July. The return trip would take them home just before the ice set in again. At the other end of the line the voyageurs carried the beaver pelts by land and water equal distances to the exchange point and then returned before the early autumn snows. It was a hard life that went on for generations.

The fur trade ended in the mid-nineteenth century when fashions throughout the world changed. Silk became the "in" thing and the demand for beaver fur dropped dramatically. And none too soon. No real attempt had been made to repopulate the beaver; it nearly became extinct. And so did the voyageur. Washington Irving wrote of them:

"Their glory is departed. They are no longer lords of our internal seas and the great navigators of the wilderness. Some of them may still occasionally be seen coasting the lower lakes with their frail barks, and pitching their camps and lighting their fires upon the shore; but their range is fast contracting to those remote waters and shallow, obstructed rivers unvisited by the steamboats. In the course of years they will gradually disappear; their songs will die away like the echoes they once awakened, and the Canadian voyageurs will become a forgotten race, or remembered, like their associates, the Indians, among the poetical images of past time, and as themes for local and romantic associations."

Perhaps the gutsy, fun-loving, and industrious voyageur has finally found his place in history, but, one might ask, why romanticize an industry that so blatantly destroyed native wildlife? The Congressional Act preserves "the outstanding scenery, geological conditions, and waterway system which constituted a part of the historic route of the Voyageurs . . . ," 219,000 acres, about 85,000 of which are water and all the rest heavily forested. Much of the land is undeveloped and accessible only by motorboat and is, in our parlance, one of those last vestiges of wilderness-America, a microcosm, in effect, of the whole northern region of the country and of the route traveled by the voyageur.

This splendid, unspoiled land is built on the most solid foundation, ancient Precambrian rock laid down billions of years ago and shaved off by giant glaciers. It is a land like no other, interwoven by waterways, lakes of all sizes and shapes, islands big and small, framed by great vertical cliffs and huge boulders dropped by the melting ice of forgotten times. One senses the strong arm of Hiawatha, moccasins of deerskin, birch-bark canoes, the wigwam of Nokomis . . . a lonely silence broken only by the occasional dip of a paddle or the

Colorful splashes of wild flowers, like the showy lady's slipper above, *peep between the park's cool tongues of greenery, and a crimson sunset floods Kabetogama Narrows, seen from the Visitor Center* left. (National Park Service Photos by Dan Ritter).

scream of a soaring eagle.

Voyageurs National Park is new – it had no previous federal protective status – and is still being developed as a full-scale park. Everything one could possibly want is here, however, and in these times it is all anyone really needs – a nature as refreshing as the spirit of the adventurer who, with but the fibers of birch bark and the determination to survive, molded an empire and opened a highway into the wilderness.

Sigurd Olson wrote in his *Reflections from the North Country:*

"It is good for us to recall the hardihood and simplicities that period represents, for we are still part of those frontiers and will survive because of what they gave us. We must solve the enormous problems that confront us, far bigger ones than we have ever known, but we face them with those sterling qualities woven into our pioneer character. Within us is an inner reserve of power and resilience because of what the frontiers did."

Isle Royale National Park

To step onto Isle Royale is to leave behind one's old self and one's old world and to begin a new exploration into the nature of life.
Napier Shelton, *The Life of Isle Royale*

No doubt there are those who flinch at the association of wolf-moose, prey-predator relationship with Isle Royale National Park, so overworked and overtold is the story. Yet it is, in the words of Michael Frome, "a dramatic national park saga."

Rather than so often studying the cause of wildlife extinction, scientists' seeming misfortune, here on Isle Royale man has witnessed in modern times an evolution of migration, growth and dissipation and behavioral habits of two native North American mammals. The island is a laboratory.

This marvelous wilderness sanctuary lies just fifteen miles off Canada, in Lake Superior. Its close proximity to the mainland, yet its isolation and size – forty-five miles long, nine miles wide – has made it just right for a microcosm of nature's balance – neat and compact for a close look.

A 1905 Michigan Biological Survey of Isle Royale (the island is within the boundaries of Michigan) shows not a single moose on the island – lots of other wildlife, but no moose – nor can a wolf be found listed. Sometime after 1905, some think the winter of 1912 when the lake froze, a family of moose wandered across the ice. Within a short time the population had doubled, and so on, and so on, until the mid-thirties when some three thousand were literally starving to death. There simply was not enough browse, or food, to sustain a herd this size. Many died in 1933, and again in 1936 when fire burned a quarter of the island; the herd dropped to four hundred.

Vegetation soon renewed and so the moose, until about 1948, when another of those mysterious and unseen things happened that aided nature in its "perfect balance." Lake Superior froze again, and this time the wolf came to the island for the first time. The prey-predator relationship among wildlife took on a new dimension. The wolves, only about twenty or so, now keep the moose herd at just the right level to survive, and nearly every phase of the behavior of these two animals is studied with care. They both thrive in the most ideal conditions. And so does man.

Isle Royale National Park is a rock fortress, capped by dense forests and peppered, it seems, with lakes, streams, and hundreds of little off-shore islands. It has been called the nearest thing to a true wilderness we have outside of Alaska, but it has not by any means missed the world of man. There was a time, before it became a park in 1940, when human ramblings took their toll.

During the beaver-trapping days of the voyageurs, there were six trading posts here; the Hudson's Bay

Forcibly contrasted with Isle Royale's scenic autumnal beauty below right, *and the melancholy loveliness of mist-shrouded Tobin Harbor* right, *is the scene* above as, *on the hard-packed snow, predatory wolves feed on the carcass of an ill-fated moose – necessary in the delicate counterpoise of nature that is an essential part of the park's unique ecological balance.* (National Park Service Photos).

Company had one or two, the others belonging to the American Fur Company. In the nineteenth century copper mining brought hundreds from the mainlands, Canada, and Michigan; hundreds who simply followed the footsteps of early natives whose open pits gave clues to the element found nowhere around this country. Much of the virgin forest was burned away to expose the precious metal. But, as with the wildlife, the wilderness has sought its balance; and the island today is much as it was when first discovered.

The foundation of Isle Royale is lava dating some 1.2 million years, layers of lava flows that tilted and dipped at angles. It is the gentle peaks of these strata, jutting upwards through the lake, that form the island. Glacial ice – billions of tons of it – depressed most of this, but as the ice melted and land rebounded, so to speak, Isle Royale began to "emerge." It continues to do so at the rate of about a foot or more each century. Here and there can be seen previous shorelines marked by gravel and smooth, rounded stones.

This is just one of the fascinating mysteries cloaked by the isolation of this quiet place in the north country. Isle Royale is one of nature's artifacts, large enough to be a haven for those who seek solitude under most primitive conditions, small enough to be seen as a living tool in understanding life itself.

Acadia National Park

Acadia... where can you find anything in our country to match these mountains that come down to the ocean, these granite cliffs alongside which the biggest ships could ride, these bays dotted with lovely islets clothed in hardwood and hemlock, altogether such a sweep of rugged coastline as has no parallel from Florida to the Canadian provinces? ... Everything is here to rejoice the soul of the human visitor...
Freeman Tilden, *The National Parks*

Early one autumn morning during World War II, it is said, a German submarine slipped quietly into Frenchman Bay, past Bar Harbor on Mount Desert Island and, someplace in the deep waters along this Maine coastline, set three spies off in a rubber raft toward the rocky shore. The story is apocryphal; but if a U-boat commander did venture into this harbor, he knew exactly what he was doing. The waters along Maine's coast are deep; Somes Sound, which penetrates Mount Desert Island, is a fjord that is at once inviting and yet hostile in welcome.

Sunrise touches the United States first here at Acadia National Park in Maine, a place where, in contrast to the delicate morning light and the surrounding, soft fingers of fog, the irresistible sea clashes harshly with an immovable, rocky coastline. By comparison, Acadia is one of the smaller national parks, but its size makes it no less important in the chain of great natural areas held in preservation by the nation. As a matter of fact, it is the size that makes it such a special place: the last vestige of the 'rock-bound coast of Maine'. There is really nothing quite like it along the Atlantic and no other place in the East where the geological story is so closely linked to glaciers and the sea. Nor is there another park on this coast where the forces of nature are so blatantly obvious.

From about Portland to the St. Croix River, which separates Maine from New Brunswick – perhaps 185 miles as the crow flies – there are some 2,500 tortuous miles of jagged shoreline: inlets, coves, bays, and sounds of fortress-like granite cliffs and boulder-strewn beaches. Only a small part of this is Acadia: Mount Desert Island, Isle au Haut, and the tip of Schoodic Peninsula – some 38,000 acres in all. But nature's relentless shaping, defining, and redefining of this land is nowhere better demonstrated than right here.

Scientists speculate that Acadia had several lives before the great Ice Age, times when it was covered by the sea, times much warmer when lava flowed and the land was molded into mountains and valleys, times when the rocks were formed and trees grew and even life itself began to crawl and fly about. It was the time of gigantic glaciers, however, that created most of what we see today – glaciers of about seventy thousand years ago. That's almost like yesterday on the geological clock.

It was in 1837 that Swiss naturalist Louis Agassiz

first talked about glaciers covering northern Europe. When he came to this country and saw Mount Desert Island in 1846, he soon made comparisons and announced that America, too, had once been covered with ice, and that it may have been glaciers nine thousand feet thick that had carved this coastline. As in Europe, the evidence was startling; and while Agassiz's theories were slow in acceptance, we now know them to be true.

At one time this land was much higher, the coast much farther out to sea. Glaciers from the north carved much of it away; and as the ice melted and the sea rose, what were once river valleys and stream beds were filled by the ocean; mountain tops became islands. In essence, the weight of the ice (a single acre, one mile thick, may have weighed seven million tons) and its constant movement depressed and wore down the land and carried the debris to the sea. As the ocean moved in, it literally drowned the coast. And today, in a never-ending geologic evolution, the sea and the land continue their battle – enormous energy unleashed in tides that batter and carve and change.

Set amid the chiseled, granite cliffs, the Bass Harbor Headlight below *and seen* overleaf *dramatically silhouetted against the setting sun, is a welcoming sentinel to mariners when fog belies the dangerous coastline.*

Behind the golden tints of fall foliage nestle the Hamilton Laboratory Farm Buildings above.

At Thunder Hole, for example, rushing tides lash at a narrow chasm of rock with mighty, near-sonic booms, trying desperately, it seems, to claim even more of the land. Huge boulders torn away by the sea are thrown back like pebbles. At Baker Island giant slabs of granite are cracked and ripped away as if by some powerful machine and carried away only to be flung back to rebuild the shoreline somewhere else.

Lest Acadia be imagined a place of violence, a walk only yards from the shore will quickly dispel that. The land is hospitable, pristine, and often within only a step or tree-trunk from the lofty geysers created by the tides.

First established as Lafayette National Park in 1919, Acadia, renamed in 1929, was the first national park in the East and the only one in New England. Most of the park is on Mount Desert Island, where for many years the property was owned by "summer residents". It was this group of people, bent on protecting the wilderness, that created the park by giving their land to the federal government. The boundaries are as jagged as the shore, but this is a park that has grown and developed from within. Cadillac Mountain, 1,530 feet, is the highest point on the Atlantic coast. Below it lies Frenchman Bay and the old resort town of Bar Harbor.

This is a land that appeals to the senses, lures one back to the primitive, and inspires the creative minds of poets and artists and photographers. Mount Desert Island alone is a world unto itself, a world unchanged since the ice left, recycling itself in nature's way and barely touched by man's so-called civilization. Scattered about the island are dozens of lakes and ponds filled with trout, salmon, and bass, and surrounded by evergreen forests of balsam fir and red spruce. Wildlife abounds, from the porpoises that glide through the harbors to the white-tailed deer and red fox that roam the forest.

There are other primitive areas here in the East and in the West, but there is something special about Acadia. Some of that, of course, is the geological clock so present. The glaciers departed just a few days ago, relatively speaking, and that sort of tickles the imagination. But there is a moodiness about this place that sets it apart from others. There are times when you can be as alone and remote as any human on earth. When the warm Gulf Stream flowing north in the Atlantic meets the cold Labrador Current just off the coast, water moisture condenses into a thick fog that drifts in and envelops the outer islands and the shore of Mount Desert. It closes down fishing and sends vacationers inside; but if you are out along the many trails and pathways in the park, the fog singles you out, isolates you from the world, echoing your thoughts to the innermost soul.

On Acadia it is a time for reflection; the clock stands still as only the roar and crash of the ocean tells of the outside. The rocky shore welcomes the day, then holds it in captivity while man stumbles and ponders and then decides that this is a place of well-being.

13

Shenandoah National Park

I ain't so crazy about leavin' these hills, but I never believed in bein' agin' the government. I signed the papers they asked me.... I allus said these hills would be the heart of the world.

Hezekiah Lam

Hezekiah Lam was eighty-five the day Franklin D. Roosevelt dedicated Shenandoah National Park. He had lived a long and hard, and no doubt happy and content, life within the shadows of these Blue Ridge Mountains.

Now, that life had come to an end. Properties had been condemned, families moved. Some went happily, others fought to stay. It was unprecedented, but it was done. "I never believed in bein' agin' the government," Lam had said, but he probably never really understood what it was all about, or, for that matter, Roosevelt's words that day in 1936: "In every part of the country . . . [we] are engaged in preserving and developing our heritage of natural resources."

The winning back of Shenandoah – winning back rather than saving, for, like the Great Smokies, much of it was already lost – was a long and protracted battle; some forty years in fact if one considers the earliest preservation movements in Virginia.

The impact pre-Europeans made on this land of the Blue Ridge Mountains was negligible, but that native Americans were here as far back as ten thousand years ago is certain. Their burial mounds and artifacts have been found on both sides of the mountains. They fished and hunted and no doubt farmed in some manner. They were Siouan, Monacau, and Manahoacs, and they cleared and burned and they killed for food, but they were small in number and left little sign of destruction. And by the time of the white man, the Indian was gone.

John Lederer, a German Native, was the first white man to venture into the Blue Ridge. That was 1669. It would be another fifty-five years before settlement would come, but when it came in 1725-1730, it came in full force, and from that day the Shenandoah Valley and the Blue Ridge Mountains were doomed to a sad and untimely demise. By the mid-nineteenth century and the Civil War, the wildlife was gone, the timberland stripped bare, and the precious, thin soil of the mountains eroded to a mere shell.

The valley was settled first, and the farms were successful and profitable, but as more and more pioneers came from eastern Virginia and south from Pennsylvania, land became scarce and families moved up the slopes of the mountains. Soon the forests were gone and the chestnut tree, that marvelous old American chestnut, disappeared. The copper, iron, and manganese miners came and went, and the timber business flourished briefly and then moved on, and the mountain folk, many of whom were totally uneducated, suffered the blight of the whirlwind exploitation.

As day fades, a pink-washed sky hangs above the lonely landscape of Big Meadows above, *while from Skyline Drive at Sawmill Ridge* right, *a sea of massed green foliage fades towards the horizon. The golden colors of fall contrast with an early dusting of snow* above right *to create an idyllic, timeless scene.*

The land was unproductive, the scars of the expanding empire bearing mute testimony to a waste of some of *their* most valuable resources.

In the late-nineteenth century a new breed of mountain people came to the Blue Ridge, people who appreciated natural beauty, people who came to play and decry the despoliation. Some of them caught the national park idea from George Freeman Pollock, owner of Skyland Resort and five thousand acres of mountain top, who proposed a preserve here within driving distance of the nation's capital. Although Pollock's preachings were contagious, there was the question of money to buy private land, land owned by families for generations. Virginians, more than twenty-four thousand of them, liked the idea and contributed $1.3 million; the Virginia Legislature added another million and after eleven years of litigation and condemnations, Shenandoah National Park was created.

The forests have taken a long time to recover, indeed they are not fully recovered yet, but this is a splendid three hundred square miles of gentle wilderness where three million people each year renew some faith in nature. They travel the 105 miles of the Skyline Drive, oblivious of the scars still just beyond the roadway and the bitter struggles to provide enough acreage to lend some grace and dignity once again to the old Blue Ridge.

Today, the chestnut fights against the age-old and mysterious disease introduced from Asia in 1900, the disease that finally all but wiped it out, and here and there survives for a few years. Wildlife – not the bison or wolf or elk or the marvelous passenger pigeon who have passed on – are slowly and timidly returning to re-establish a habitat.

It is a new breed of outdoorsmen who now come to the Blue Ridge. This is their one touch of the earth, the rock, the wildflower, the sky. Shenandoah is a "recycled park," once nearly lost and now saved. Its rocks are billions of years old, a foundation of lava flows and crustal upheavals that date to a time when continents shifted and folded and wrinkled. But Shenandoah is also new and bright and warm and friendly. Shenandoah is a re-creation of life that only man in an age of threatened environments can understand and appreciate.

Mammoth Cave National Park

It's not much of a house, but we've got one hell of a basement.
Traditional Flint Ridge greeting.
The Longest Cave

Floyd Collins died on February 16, 1925, something of a hero. He did not want it that way, had never planned it that way, but he died with his picture on the front page of newspapers across the country and with his name on the lips of millions of Americans who had never been to Kentucky and who had only the vaguest image of the inside of a cave. Floyd is a legend now, but for 18 days in the winter of '25 he was real – "good copy," as a reporter might say, a press agent's dream.

Floyd Collins was nobody special except to the people of Warren County, Kentucky. who knew him as a cave explorer; an extraordinary caver obsessed with finding a "secret entrance" to the great Mammoth Cave and with making a fortune. In January 1925, Floyd set out to explore Sand Cave on the narrow bridge of land between Flint Ridge and Mammoth Cave Ridge, south of Bowling Green. He was the best in the business and, although he had discovered several caves around there and had commercialized one, Crystal Cave, none of the locations had brought him much money. Rival caves were attracting tourists on their way to Mammoth, but Crystal was too far away. Floyd wanted to be the *first* to catch the visitor's eye; Sand Cave was just right.

Throughout January he dug and scraped and moved rocks and slowly inched his way back through the earth from one passageway to another, each step of the way giving him confidence that soon he would be a rich man. Sometime around the last day of January he was cleaning out a crawlway when a fifty-pound rock fell across his ankle and pinned him to the floor of the cave.

Confident that someone would come to his rescue, Floyd waited. The next morning a friend came, then his brothers, and later his father, himself a caving expert. But Floyd's body filled the crawlway, and no one could get to the rock. It looked bad. By the end of the day the news had gone out that Floyd Collins was trapped in Sand Cave.

News was slow that February 1925, and the Collins story made headlines. The February 2 edition of the *Washington Post* carried a boxed lead: "Man, foot held by rock in cave, is facing death." It shared the front page with a prediction from Secretary of War Curtis Wilbur that a "devastating gas" would wipe out both sides in the next world war. That same day Leonard Sepalla, famed "sleigh musher of the North," was in the final miles of a mercy mission to Nome, Alaska; he was carrying a precious supply of diphtheria serum.

William "Skeets" Miller, a reporter for the Louisville *Courier Journal* raced to Cave City and volunteered his services in Floyd's rescue. He was a small

man and could fit into tight places and, besides, he wanted the story. Miller immediately began filing his reports, and the Associated Press picked them up and sent them all over the country. For a short time Miller was actually in charge of the operations, moving into tiny openings, talking with Floyd, and helping to move out the debris. By February 4 Miller's name was on the front pages and so was Floyd's picture.

On February 5, Attorney General Harlan Fiske Stone was appointed to the Supreme Court, and a Congressional committee was investigating the "sudden increase in the price of gasoline," but in Cave City, Kentucky, Homer Collins was offering $500 to anyone who could rescue his brother. Another $500 was put up by the crowd that had gathered at Sand Cave. And it was a huge crowd. First came concerned neighbors, then the townspeople, and then people from all over the country. On February 6 the *Washington Post* reported "hundreds;" two days later there were "thousands." On the 9th there was a "special to the *Post*" report that 10,000 had collected in the "first real Sunday crowd." Parson Jim Hamilton conducted church services that morning amidst a "country fair atmosphere" that would go on for the next ten days. Hamburgers were twenty-five cents; vendors hawked hot dogs, balloons, apples, and soda pop; and there was a three-dollar taxi service to and from town.

"Spectators took a morbid peep at this rock prison," the *Post* said. "After an hour or two of staring, they came back and sat in their flivvers to watch until torch lights lasted into the night." Rumors circulated that first Floyd was rescued and would soon be out, then he was dead, and then, that it was all just a publicity stunt for Crystal Cave. It was, of course, much more serious than that, but the Collins family was not above taking advantage of the crowd. During all of this, Floyd's father walked through the crowd passing out leaflets advertising visits to Crystal Cave at "$2 a trip."

The attempts to save Floyd became more daring as time went on. Everyone had a plan, the most promising of which was a shaft drilled from above. Then the ceiling of the cave collapsed and cut Floyd off from all but the engineers on top who frantically pressed down. On the 16th, when the workers finally reached him, Floyd was dead. Newspapers across the nation and in Europe carried banner headlines.

At this point it seemed that nothing could be more bizarre than Floyd's last days, but the events that followed exceeded even the macabre. Floyd wanted to be buried where he fell and his friends complied. The passageway was sealed in concrete. But two months later Floyd's brother, Lee, decided on a proper burial and had the tomb opened. The body was embalmed and reburied near Crystal Cave.

Two years later Lee decided to sell Crystal Cave. Harry Thomas, the man who bought it, had already successfully operated two commercial caves, but Crystal was something special . . . It was already a drawing card because Floyd Collins had discovered it, but what if . . . what if Floyd were *buried* there? Somehow the Collins family agreed. Thomas had Floyd exhumed and placed in the "Grand Canyon," the large entrance room to Crystal, in a glass-covered coffin. Now called "Floyd Collins' Crystal Cave," the newest Cave City attraction was sensational. Thousands filed by Floyd's body while guides told stories about "the world's greatest cave explorer." And there was much more to satisfy the public's morbid curiosity, but . . . that's better left to the public's morbid curiosity.

Overnight Floyd Collins became the country's most famous caver. The publicity he unwittingly generated was worth millions to this Kentucky valley and, in a sense, he still shares in all that he created. But Floyd is only a small part of the Mammoth Cave story that spans 200 years of written history and probably as much as three thousand years of history known only by archeological findings.

Indians lived in the Mammoth Cave area as early as 1,000 B.C., and there is very good evidence that they knew about the cave and used it; "Lost John," a mummified "miner" discovered in 1935, was digging for gypsum some 2,300 years ago when a huge boulder crushed him to death. Like Floyd Collins his remains became a tourist attraction until the better senses of the National Park Service put him away.

The first known white man to enter Mammoth Cave was Valentine Simons, in 1798, although he was undoubtedly preceded by many others. Simons bought the land, some two hundred acres, and it was registered in his name at the county courthouse. He mined saltpeter – that's about all the cave was good for in its earliest years – until about 1816 when some travelers began stopping by.

The tourist business did not really begin until the first explorations and mapping in the 1830's, but the cave was still off the "beaten path" and seldom seen. Then in 1838, Franklin Gorin, who it was said, was the first white man born in this region, bought the cave and set one of his slaves, Stephen Bishop, to exploring. Before he died in 1857, Bishop had become America's first great cave explorer. He had seen and mapped more than eight miles of passageways, rooms, streams and rivers, and had gained an international reputation.

What Bishop and his many followers saw was a geological phenomenon quite unlike any in the world, and it attracted the curious from all over, even without the benefit of Floyd Collins; Jenny Lind once gave a concert there, Edwin Booth recited Shakespeare, and even Jesse James held up the old Mammoth stage filled with tourists and relieved them of a few hundred dollars. Today the curious still come to see what water and time have created.

Some 240 million years ago, the seas that covered what is now west-central Kentucky deposited layer-upon-layer of mud, shells, and sand. All of these hardened into the limestone and sandstone we see today. Then as the land around uplifted, the seas drained away, seeping through cracks in the earth's crust and eroding away the underground stone. Millions of years of this abrasive action created hundreds of caves and passageways, and from the ceilings, where the ground-water has percolated through, a myriad colorful stalactites.

One hundred and fifty miles of Mammoth Cave have been explored, and speleologists, that marvelous breed of underground enthusiasts, believe that there may be hundreds more that link this great system to others in this section of the country. The most sought-after and challenging connection was made in 1972 when the Mammoth and nearby Flint Ridge Cave systems were linked by a spunky team of five people who, after a night of some of the most difficult caving, discovered a previously unsurveyed route. It was the top of Everest in the caving world and once again brought Warren County, Kentucky, to the front pages.

"Whether he [Floyd Collins] ever tried to find connections between the big caves does not matter," wrote Roger Brucker and Richard Watson. "He was a caver. He must have thought about it. And the exploration that had led to all the connections in the last twenty years had been made following the footsteps of Floyd Collins."

Mammoth Cave became a national park in 1926 after years of controversy over land acquisitions, and attitudes in these Kentucky hills still reflect the bitter disputes between the federal government and private enterprise. Fortunately for all, nature, at least here, fails to acknowledge man's follies. This is a world unto itself: a room as high as a twenty-story building; delicate, flower-like gypsum crystals; 150 miles of cave on five levels; all spectacular, all inspiring, and preserved for all to enjoy.

Floyd Collins still lies in state in Crystal Cave. Crystal is closed to the public, but no doubt Floyd's spirit explores, wandering endlessly . . . endlessly.

Beavers previous page *occupy much of their time in and around Mammoth Cave Park's rivers* below left. *The park's main attraction, however, is undoubtedly the incredible network of caves from which it takes its name. Among its many features are:* Limestone Bluffs *above left,* Roaring River *above,* Thorp's Pit *below and* Kentucky Avenue *right.* (National Park Service Photos).

Great Smoky Mountains National Park

We should be impressed by the beauty and fragility of the dynamic balance that has been preserved for so many hundreds of millions of years during which life has persisted on earth. And we should especially appreciate the shortness of our tenure on earth and use the powers we have so recently assumed to perpetuate, not destroy, the balance.
Eliot Porter, *Appalachian Wilderness*

It seems certain now that some of the first humans to inhabit the North American continent passed through the southern Appalachian Mountains. Most likely, too, "they stayed a spell," as today's mountain people might say, for here and there those nomadic tribes of some fifteen thousand years ago left scraps of intriguing evidence. Ethnologists believe they may also have left behind an even greater legacy: one of the largest and most stable of America's early societies, the Cherokee.

If this is true, then the Great Smoky Mountains may be the oldest continuously inhabited area of the country. There was no great drought or violent volcanic eruptions to drive this civilization away. They hunted and farmed and thrived in what must surely have been their "Garden of Eden." But, alas, as years went by, the Cherokee was nearly destroyed and *Shaconage,* "the place of the blue smoke," their home for at least a thousand years of recorded time, nearly lost.

The Appalachians are about 400 million years old; that's probably three times older than the Rocky Mountains. There was much earth activity before that and certainly much later, but that seems to be about the time of the "mountain making" in the East. No one knows precisely when the first plants and trees began to root but it was sometime after the last glacial period. All of that time plotted on the face of a rule stretches nearly to the end. The tragedies of the Smokies came in that last fraction of an inch, between the early 1800's and 1940 when the Great Smoky Mountain National Park was established.

It was the first European settlers who set in motion the chain of events that forecast this land's demise; and it was their descendants, who, in the waning hours, wrested it from destruction and saved it.

The Great Smokies are not as delicate as the grassy ocean of the Everglades or as tough as the granite peaks of Yosemite, but like these other great preserves, they have no immunity from the arrogant tools of man. Aldo Leopold wrote: "When some remote ancestor of ours invented the shovel, he became a giver; he could plant a tree. And when the axe was invented, he became a taker; he could chop it down." No doubt the axe·came first. It did in the Smokies and sixty-percent of this primeval forest fell before the shovel began to replenish.

Man's most dangerous tool, the gun, was the first to enter these mountains, and the Cherokee was the first to fall. The Smokies was their home; their first village,

A Le Conte Creek waterfall above *tumbles its way around massive boulders.*
Mingus Mill right, *in the Great Smoky Mountains' foothills, once provided ground meal for the early pioneers.*

Kituwha, was located just inside the present park boundary, near Bryson City, North Carolina. It was these people who named the mountains, and it was they who built a nation long before European influence. Such a culture, however advanced, could offer little resistance against the overwhelming tide of English, Scots-Irish, and German settlers who, following the Revolution, pressed toward the fertile lands of the western frontier. By 1828, their land confiscated, their government voided, and with guns to their backs, the Cherokee succumbed, and in one of the darkest moments of American history, were marched off to what is now Oklahoma.

The Indian had never really tamed this great wilderness, but it was a compatible relationship; he was small in number with few needs for survival and thus made little mark on the land. Not so his conqueror. By the 1850's the valleys and coves had been claimed, fields stripped of rocks and trees, and mountaintops cleared for pasture. Another kind of civilization moved in, and it is still there.

Life in the Smoky Mountains was isolated at first, bare of all but the most essential: a cabin, a spring, oxen for the plow, a few chickens, a cow, if fortunate, and a spinning wheel and rifle. Religion and music became the staples of a simple, unadorned life that forged small communities and knitted several cultures into one. The "mountain people" survived in a world all their own. They liked it that way, and they kept it that way, a private vision of freedom, independence, settlement; a self-sufficient permanence.

These were an exuberant people, courageous and strong and defiant, who could be at the same time generous and violent. They lived hard and they died hard, generation after generation. Life styles changed but little through the years; mail service came, roads linked valleys, and transportation evolved, but customs and traditions clung tenaciously to the hills.

Then at the turn of the century the second tragedy of the Smokies began when the Little River Lumber Company bought 8,600 acres of timberland. Systematically, for the next twenty years, the Smokies were mined with no regard for the future. Two-thirds of the forest, trees that had stood for centuries, was cleared to satisfy the insatiable building appetite of the eastern coastal cities. Streams were dammed and then unleashed to carry logs away to the mills; railroads were cut through; mill towns grew; other lumber companies moved in and the industry spread. And with all this, the mountain people changed. They sold their land and their goods and stood by as first the saw and axe and then nature began to turn this once lush, green country, where streams tumbled through the hills and wildlife grazed placidly in the meadows, into a scarred, barren wasteland. Fires jumped from cut to cut; rains washed the unprotected topsoil down and mountains literally slid away leaving behind the ancient rock from eons ago. Still, by 1923, there was just enough timber left to make it worth the effort to preserve, in spite of it all, the largest virgin forest in the East.

The beginnings of Great Smoky Mountains National Park is the classic tale of conservation versus industry versus homesteader. It is not a pleasant story, nor can its final chapter ever indicate all that went before. Preservation money was slow in coming, and the well-entrenched families and lumber companies fought the sale of land that continued to yield a living. But private citizens of Tennessee and North Carolina, determined to protect the last vestiges of this wilderness, proposed a national park and fought hard to get it. More than six thousand individual parcels of land comprised the proposed park, and it took millions of dollars and many years of emotionally-charged negotiations to make it a reality. The park was finally established in 1934.

The Great Smokies are a microcosm of the geological and human histories of this nation: the two, man and nature, intertwined in an inexorable struggle against each other. First, the mountains, hundreds of millions of years of building and sculpturing, and that still goes on as the summers and winters bend and stretch the earth's crust and imperceptibly move things about. Then, man, at first gently and then harshly, altered the landscape and the wildlife that roamed the forest.

But this land belies what has happened. The mountains, seemingly, continue to sleep peacefully, surrounded by that mysterious blue haze that so struck the first Indians. The brilliant display of nature – there are 130 native trees, more than in all of Europe, and more than 1,300 varieties of flowering plants – shields the scars of the past century and deludes the mind. There are more than one-half million acres in the park, and forty percent of it is as it was when the Cherokee first came. The wildlife – nearly dissipated by the time the park was established – is now protected and coming back. There are about 200 species of birds, 50 species of mammals, 40 of reptiles, and 70 of fish. And, of course, the black bear, that engaging, would-be clown, is the most popular animal in the park. Visitors can drink in the mountain culture and all the rest that the mountains have to offer, but the one thing they will remember most is the bear.

And the Cherokee is back. (Part of the tribe never left. About a thousand secreted themselves in the most remote areas of the mountains and survived.) The U.S. Government, some years after that terrible "trail of tears" to Oklahoma, permitted the tribe to return and reclaim some of their homeland. Today the proud and patient Cherokee lives on the Qualla Reservation, once again in the shadow of "the place of blue smoke."

The Great Smoky Mountains are a metaphor for nature. The park's 522,000 acres is seventy-five percent wilderness; its 800 miles of trails, 700 miles of streams, and sixteen peaks of over 6,000 feet are a paradise for those who love nature. And they come every year, nine million strong. This is the most visited of all national parks.

Fallen trees left *in a stream, crossed by a wooden bridge on the path to Chimney Tops lend an essential air of nature's cycle of renewal to this part of the Great Smoky Mountains National Park.*

Typical of many such scenes in the park is the view of the cascading stream right *and Little River* overleaf.

Mist hangs between the tree-covered mountain slopes above *seen from Newfound Gap Road.*

The towering Chimney Tops below *have an elevation of 4,755 feet and have become almost the 'trade-mark' of the park.*

There are many vantage points from which to view the ever-changing and varied aspects of the Great Smoky Mountains. Top left and bottom left are views from Newfound Gap Road; center left from Chimney Tops, and above from Blue Ridge Parkway.

Below are shown the tumbling waters of the Little River, and right is a tranquil scene at Cades Cove.

To find real peace of mind it would be hard to better the soothing, calming effects of water as it tumbles and flows over falls, makes its way over and around rocks and boulders or between the tree-lined banks of rivers and streams, of which there are several hundred miles in the Great Smoky Mountains National Park.
Near the park's entrance is Oconaluftee River above and below; left and bottom right Little River; top right The Sinks, on the Little River Road and center right the popular Laurel Falls.

Grotto Falls above *is one of the most beautiful in the park, reached by an easy hike of over two miles along the Nature Trail leading from Roaring Fork* below.

Right is a densely-wooded stream on the path to Chimney Tops and below right *fall colors glow softly in the evening sun at Cades Cove, where tall trees* left *stand like sentinels.*

Everglades National Park

I somehow feel sure…that what does remain of the Everglades will always be there, for how much poorer America would be without it.
Michael Frome, *The National Parks*

No other natural area in the National Park System, and perhaps the whole of the United States, is so delicately balanced between survival and destruction as the Everglades of Florida. And yet it has been abused by man and man's follies more than any other. Some speculate that if we ever lose a national park, it will probably be the Everglades, not through development – the boundaries are firmly fixed and the land protected from the bulldozer forever – but from the steady tipping of the ecological scales.

The Everglades is a broad, flat river of fresh water that flows from Lake Okeechobee in central Florida 120 miles south to Florida Bay and the Gulf of Mexico. It has done so since time unknown, an endless "river of grass" that moves so imperceptively slowly it seems to stand still. The life it once cradled and nourished may have been the most abundant anywhere, an incredible array of nature which, even before man came to Florida, clung tenaciously to a shallow foothold.

Southern Florida is low country; the highest point in the state, in the northern panhandle, is only 345 fee above sea level. Here in the Everglades land height is measured in inches. It was not always like this. Several times in the past million or so years, it seems, the sea level between glacial periods left this peninsula of ancient limestone high and dry. As glaciers melted, the sea rose and the land was once again covered. During these remote periods ridges of limestone were built along the outer perimeters of the now Florida shape, thus creating a shallow bowl effect.

This was the setting for the creation of the Everglades – a limestone basin, tilted slightly to the south and west, and lined with layers of peat, decayed grass and marsh plants, which collected the abundant, summer rainfall (about sixty inches a year) and set it flowing, gently, to the sea.

Essentially this is what the Everglades is today . . . except some changes have been made that for the past seventy years have seriously jeopardized the existence of this subtropical wonderland. Man!

Both coasts of Florida were inhabited by Indians when explorers arrived in the early 1500's. Some say they were descendants of the ancient civilizations of Mexico and Peru. Whatever they were, by the late eighteenth century they had disappeared, leaving behind only their burial mounds as evidence of their tribes. During the early 1800's purge of the Creek Confederation in the southern states, many from these tribes took refuge in the Florida Everglades and became known as the Seminoles. Even here they were not beyond the arm of military pursuers, but they

survived and have lived quietly and unobtrusively, and nearly forgotten, since.

The white man "discovered" Florida around the turn of the century. One of his "discoveries" was that by drawing water from the Everglades, the resulting soil, thin as it was, could be farmed. Dikes were laid around Lake Okeechobee, canals were built and fresh water let to the sea, Miami was founded on the east coast, and . . . the race was on. But somewhere along the way the developers met themselves coming around the bend. Okeechobee flooded and spilled and thousands died, the fine organic soil oxidized and the peat base burned, salt water filtered in to fill the fresh water vacuum, and the Everglades began to dry up in the drought season –

Willow Head Fresh Water Slough, Anhinga Trail below, *Cypress Mangrove Swamp, Tamiami Trail* right, *and water hyacinths* overleaf *are part of the superb exhibits to be seen in the Everglades' magnificent aquatic setting.*

wildlife and plants and trees with it. The whole fragile ecological system of southern Florida had been turned upside down. It was a disaster!

One of the key factors in upsetting nature's balance in the Everglades, and, oddly enough, the same in spurring preservation movements, was, like beaver-trapping in the northwest, the fashion industry. Some of the early Florida settlers found that around 1886 there was a very profitable market in the plumes of tropical birds, primarily the herons and snowy and great egrets. The New York millinery industry paid handsome prices for these feathers . . . and the Everglades was a forest of herons and egrets. Almost overnight business boomed. Hunters galore pursued nesting places with a vengeance until by 1905 game wardens were being murdered and the herons and egrets had all but disappeared.

The Audubon Society stepped in to protect the birds. This was followed by other conservation organizations who sought just to preserve what was left of the rapidly diminishing ecological system. By 1916 a small section of the Everglades was set aside as a state park. Congress authorized Everglades National Park in 1934; it was formally established in 1947.

Only one-seventh of the Everglades is within park boundaries, about 1.4 million acres, and though it is still beseiged on all sides by man-made water problems, its legislated borders have given time . . . precious time in a struggle for survival.

The Everglades is a certain kind of magic. Both ugly and beautiful, this magic – a sense of mystery and discovery – transcends the absolutes, the complexities, the disjointed and calamitous events that nearly destroyed and still threatens. Here is a tropical life blended with the temperate climate zone, where the nature of the mid-Atlantic states meets the species of the Caribbean in a rare setting of conflicts and contrasts.

The once endangered alligator is now making a comeback; fifty pairs of southern bald eagles balance somewhat tenuously on the endangered species list; the Florida panther (cougar) may not make it another century. Some birds and mammals will never be seen again in the Everglades. The boundaries have come too late.

Life in the Everglades hangs by a tiny thread. Man's progress, the constantly growing cities, his persistent invasion of nature's sanctuary . . . all of this tugs at one end, while at the other the delicate web dangles, patiently waiting.

Everglades National Park is a refuge . . . it can be a refuge for man if he only stops and tries to understand.

A young alligator basks in the Florida sun on a branch at the water's edge left.

Cypress trees below *reach high into the sky above their swamp-grown roots* overleaf.

Many species of wildlife that were once endangered now thrive in the delicate ecological balance of the Everglades.

Alligators are now a commoner sight as they lurk in and around the waters that also provide a home for numerous other creatures such as the little blue heron below *and the limpkin* bottom left.

Virgin Islands National Park

Three miles westward from St. Thomas, across the flashing blue waters of Pillsbury Sound, lies St. John, the smallest, most romantic and best-beloved of the Virgin Isles. . . . It is as wild, detached and primitive as if it were lost somewhere on the rim of an unknown sea.

Hamilton Cochran

This nation has been inordinately fortunate in real estate investments. If you consider the twenty-four dollars for Manhattan a valid sale, it was a good deal. No less so was Thomas Jefferson's crafty and secret purchase of the Louisiana Territory from Napoleon in 1803 for $16 million; the territory included one-third of the United States. And there was "Seward's folly" – Alaska. In 1867, Secretary of State William H. Seward negotiated the purchase of Alaska from Russia for $7.2 million. Both the Louisiana and Alaska deals were questioned at the time, but Jefferson and Seward have long since been vindicated.

In 1803 it seemed, at least to President Jefferson, that the security of the United States was in jeopardy when Napoleon sent French troops to quell a rebellion in Santo Domingo. Suspecting that this might be a launching base for invasion, Jefferson took advantage of time and made Napoleon an offer. It was accepted.

Similarly, in 1917, fearing that Germany had its eye on the Danish-owned Virgin Islands in the Caribbean as a naval base, the United States made another real estate deal. For $25 million we bought the three largest islands, St. Thomas, St. Croix, and St. John, and approximately fifty small islets and cays. Whether or not this altered the war in the Atlantic is questionable but, following hostilities, the purchase caused considerable debate. That was a lot of money for a group of seemingly useless islands 900 miles off shore. It was hailed as another "Seward's folly." But as with the Alaska investment, time vindicated all involved. It turned out to be a bargain.

Columbus discovered these tropical islands on his second voyage in 1493 but, as seemed his luck, he was not the first; South American Indians had been there since 300 A.D. Their village remains and petroglyphs have been found scattered about St. John.

Although there were various claims on the islands during the next two hundred years, St. Thomas and St. John were not formally settled until the early-eighteenth century and then by private, chartered companies that established sugar and cotton plantations. The Danes were the first on St. John in 1718. Within a short time they had built mills and roads and imported slaves from West Africa, but neither sugar nor cotton were suited to the islands and the industries were never really successful. The slaves rebelled in 1733. Production dropped significantly and prosperity waned until, in 1848, emancipation was proclaimed by the Danish governor, to prevent what was believed to be a major revolt. The plantation era soon ended, but the island had been virtually stripped of its native growth and wildlife.

By the time the United States took possession in 1917, some attempts were being made to reintroduce native plants and animals. Of course, by now nature has reclaimed much of the land. Evidence of the previous occupation is most noticeable in the ruins of the Danish industries. More than eighty separate estates operated at one time or another. The remains of the Annaberg, Cinnamon Bay, and Reef Bay plantations are particularly significant and while subject to the whims of the jungle, they remain as vivid and picturesque reminders of the island's past.

Interest in setting aside the entire island of St. John as a national park began in the early 1950's with the rapid growth of tourism and commercial development on nearby St. Thomas. Word had spread about this little, out-of-the-way place called St. John: white beaches, mountains rising 1,200 feet, and a year-round average temperature of 78 degrees. Only a few miles from St. Thomas, and forty miles from St. Croix, it was virtually inaccessible, so few got here to vacation. One who did, however, was Laurence Rockefeller, who contributed five thousand acres of privately owned land to the federal government. Additional land was acquired, and on August 2, 1956, Virgin Islands National Park was established. Other acreage has been acquired in recent years to enlarge the park, but it is not likely that the island itself will ever be completely within the park boundaries. St. John is only nine miles long and five miles wide; the park includes about three-quarters.

The Virgin Islands are the tips of ancient sedimentary deposits and volcanic activity and were formed much the same as other areas in the national parks. Even here the theories of plate tectonics and the moving of the earth's crust over explosive funnels in the core beneath, explains much of the land construction. What all of this has left us is a priceless tropical island of sparkling bays, brilliant beaches, and forested mountains and valleys.

Virgin Islands National Park is on what some call the heavenly side of St. John, where the trade winds and sparkling waters bring fantasies of pirates and buccaneers, where man's conflict with nature is washed fresh by the unspoiled sea, and where the solitude of a visit renews one's communication with the outside world.

Trunk Bay above right is sited on the North-West coast of the Island. Coral reefs are shown right at Leinster Bay, and overleaf all is crimsoned by the setting sun at Maho Bay.

Europa Bay left, *Salt Pond Bay* top right, *Cinnamon Bay* center right and below *and Maho Bay* bottom right *illustrate the beauty of the varied coastline of the Virgin Islands National Park.*

Much of the forest land of St. John was once cleared for raising sugarcane but it is now returning to its natural state. In areas where direct exposure to the sun has resulted in almost desert-like conditions, several species of cactus may be found, including the Turk's head top *and the candelabra-like dildo cactus* below.

Hot Springs National Park

The water in the brook was pleasantly tepid, and having no one to intrude upon my privacy, I made a profuse use of it, and wading about found that the hot water came through the slate in an an immense number of places…
G. W. Featherstonhaugh, *Excursions Through the Slave States,* 1834

One well-known guide book relegates Hot Springs National Park to its final pages stating that it barely qualifies for national park status. In comparison to the size and grandeur of Yellowstone and Yosemite and all the others, perhaps the author is right. But the national park concept, as we know it, was developed long after these ancient mineral springs in Arkansas' Ouachita Mountains were set aside by the Congress "for perpetual use and enjoyment of the people." That was in 1832; Yosemite was not discovered for another eighteen-or-so years. Hot Springs then, in many ways, is our first national park; and if our leaders were slow to apply the same protection policies elsewhere, one can take some small comfort in the knowledge that certain preservation ethics were there in our first century.

It is thought that Hernando de Soto found the springs in 1541. If he did he was probably welcomed by native Americans who had for years used these "miracle" waters as neutral ground, a place where all tribes could come without warring differences. If not "miracle" waters, at least the Indians considered the forty-some springs to be curative, and things have not changed much in the intervening years.

Hot Springs was discovered by the white man when William Dunbar and George Hunter came here in 1804. They collected some samples and, they wrote, "amused ourselves with some further experimental enquiries into the qualities of the hot waters." This brought an end to the quiet time. Within two years settlers had moved in, and the springs have been a going business since.

This was America's spa, at first a group of "wretched looking log cabins" and "a number of baths . . . made by hollowing out excavations in the rocks to which hot water is constantly flowing." But as time went on and more and more people came to seek cures for their ailments, the little village flourished. By 1856 there were seven bathhouses and a resident physician. Within another twenty years the town had a population of 3,500 and an annual tourist trade of 50,000. *Harper's New Monthly Magazine,* January 1878, described the hustle and bustle:

"On an autumn afternoon the long straggling street of the town presents a curious picture. On both sides of the thoroughfare, which is half street and half country road, teeming with the variegated population, are ranged a heterogeneous collection

Shown above and below *are the Moorish-inspired buildings lining Bath House Row;* above right *the famous color-washed facade of the Arlington Hotel facing Central Tower across curving Central Avenue, and* right *a ranger describing to two young guests the fascinating cycle of the thermal water, by one of the two Display Springs which are kept open so that visitors may see the water emerging naturally.*

of hotels, doctors' offices, stores, saloons, etc., while the bathhouses stretch in long rows on the other side of the creek. Here and there are the country wagons, drawn by gaunt mules or sleepy oxen, passing through the village, halted and bargaining with the hotel or storekeeper for the sale of their load of cotton or produce, or making desperate efforts to get out of the way of the coming horsecars . . . and everywhere the hogs, in everybody's way and under everybody's feet . . ."

"It will never be known, I suppose," wrote Freeman Tilden, "just where lies the borderline between the curative powers of the waters and the delightful social experience of exchanging symptoms and other personal history with a similarly minded group." Perhaps that's the charm of this place. Who is to dispute the infirmed who find some marvelous curing quality in this natural phenomenon? They come by the thousands and they bathe by the hour, and they somehow find that magic the Indians knew all along. It's not quite the same now as DeSoto found it, but still the waters flow.

Actually the water is quite hot, an average of 143 degrees Fahrenheit to be exact. And it is old. Old water? That sounds impossible, but the water that bubbles up from these springs – some 850,000 gallons a day – is rainwater that has seeped far into the ground long ago, heated by the earth's inner core, perhaps – no one really knows – and then forced to the surface again

through a fault in the crust. That round trip can take quite a while. Some parts of the water has been determined twenty years old, while other parts are 4,000 years old. If this is true, then some of the springs are now issuing water many times the age of the trees and plants that surround this 6,000 acre park. Like seeing the glacial parks of the North and West, a walk through the Ouachita woodland makes man seem small, almost infinitesimal, in the overall plans of nature..Hot Springs National Park is a restful place. It was to the Indian; it is again to his inheritor.

Each season brings its own reward as part of nature's bounty in the arboreal settings of Hot Springs National Park. Seen to advantage during spring, the dogwood below *fronts the densely-forested slopes of West Mountain* above *and blends with the redbud on Whittington Avenue* right, *while banks of azaleas perfume the air in The Woodland* left.

The primitive country of Big Bend National Park has been called hazardous and untameable and there is no doubt that it can be very inhospitable, yet, as the pictures on these pages show, it possesses a lonely, rugged and stark grandeur as well as much beauty, and it can certainly serve to rekindle our sense of adventure.

Guadalupe Mountains National Park

Though appearing like a forbidding fortress, the Guadalupe range, like the nearby desert, has secrets it yields only to those wise enough to look for them and with time enough to explore.

John Barnett, former park naturalist
Guadalupe Mountains National Park

Guadalupe Mountains National Park is everything that Texas is not supposed to be: a marine barrier reef, eight-thousand-foot mountains, and within the space of a few miles, a series of climate zones that range from Mexican desert to Canadian snows. It was a long time before anyone really saw or appreciated this somewhat bizarre scenery in southwest Texas. As a matter of fact, it seems that almost everyone who came near these mountains tried their best to ignore them. The very earliest Indian nomads passed through, perhaps as long as twelve thousand years ago, but evidence shows they did not tarry. Spanish explorers marching north from Mexico seemed totally unaware that the mountains existed. The first American maps of Texas charted the Guadalupes, but incorrectly, and U.S. Army survey teams consistently avoided them. It was not until 1849 that anyone took the time to acknowledge this "high range of mountains called the Sierra Guadalupes," but even then it was only in passing.

Then came John Bartlett, commissioner of the Mexican boundary survey in 1850. His was the first description that drew any public attention. Still it was another eight-or-so years before anyone other than the Apache Indian traveled these parts. In 1858 the Butterfield Overland Mail Stage began a short-lived run between St. Louis and San Francisco. Its route was just west of Guadalupe Pass. Few coaches got through without confronting Indian raids, however, and the line was soon abandoned. The Apache was master of the Guadalupes, and the white man's encroachment was not received well. Peace with the Indian came slowly and only by the persistence of the U.S. Cavalry.

At first glance one is startled by the starkness of the landscape and wonders why the mountains were not left to the Indians who somehow eked out a living here. Conditioned by Zane Grey and Hollywood, the imaginative mind sees bandits, cowboys, and cattle rustlers; and if you look up above the canyon walls, it's not difficult to conjure a chief mounted on his pony gazing out over the desert floor. In fact, that was about the limit of the inhabitants here until the early 1900's. Billy the Kid was known to hide out here, and the old Chisholm Ranch and the Lincoln County War are legendary names in these parts.

It is doubtful that any of these men of the desert knew or cared about the make-up of the Guadalupes. No one did until the geologists arrived, and then much to everyone's surprise, they found the top of these mountains to be the world's most extensive fossil

'The Pinery' above was once a regular stop for changing horses on the Celerity stagecoach run.

Looming over the surrounding desert lands stands the massive bulk of the sheer cliff of El Capitan above right.

Among the commoner plants in the park is the spiky, smooth-leaf sotol overleaf, near Hunter Peak.

organic reef. Such a phenomenon seems totally incongruous to Texas. There is no sea, no marine life, nothing with which to relate. Yet there was once here, in southwest Texas and southeast New Mexico some 250 million years ago in the Permian period, a shallow saltwater inland ocean. It had settled in an area that today might be bordered on the north by U.S. 82, on the east by Texas 18, the south by U.S. 67 and 90, and the west by Texas 54. That's stretching it a bit, but the outer perimeter of the sea can be traced by this great barrier reef in a circle of New Mexico and Texas mountains – the Guadalupes, Apache, Glass, and

Sierra Diablo. Much of the reef is buried beneath the earth, but here at Guadalupe Mountains National Park it is evident in the highest peaks in Texas.

Near the edge of this inland sea, in shallow water, lived lime-secreting algae that over eons of time built a reef not unlike that found off the coast of Queensland, Australia. As the water supply to the sea ceased to flow, the basin became stagnant and evaporated. leaving great salt flats. But the reef had been built, and despite the upheavals and cracks that occured in the earth in subsequent years, the reef remained.

Should the eye concentrate solely on the mountains, fascinating in themselves with their fossils and ancient limestone deposits, the vast ecological range of the park will be missed. Four distinct climate zones and three ecologic zones separate the basin floor from Guadalupe peak; climates ranging from that of northern Mexico to southern Canada. Cactuses and drought-resistant shrubs populate the desert-like floor, while the upper canyons and highlands are covered with ponderosa and limber pines and aspen. This wide divergence of environments has resulted in a profusion of animal life that, fortunately for all, has enjoyed nearly total protection for the past fifty years: elk, deer, bear, mountain lion, bighorn sheep, and some 200 species of birds.

Guadalupe Mountains National Park was established in 1972, for the most part through the generosity and foresight of two men who lived in and loved the mountains and who, rather simply put, wanted to see the land preserved. In 1961 Wallace Pratt, an aging oil executive who had bought a large portion of McKittrick Canyon in the Guadalupes, gave 5,632 acres to the United States. "I had been told . . . that it was the most beautiful spot in Texas," Pratt said. "So I drove a hundred-odd miles [in 1921] in an old Model T to see for myself." In 1961 Pratt found that he could no longer care for his ranch, which, even then, was called "a masterpiece of conservation and preservation." "We thought, 'My God, what's going to become of this,'" he said. "We thought somebody ought to take care of this wonderful barrier reef, protect it . . ."

A few years later another "specimen" property adjoining Pratt's became available and the national park was born. J. C. Hunter of Abilene, Texas, owned more than 70,000 acres, some 120 square miles of the Guadalupe Mountain range. For years the Hunter family had raised angora goats and had established a profitable business in mohair wool. But the Hunters had a healthy respect for the land, which like the Pratt ranch, was in pristine condition. Hunter asked $1,500,000. It was a bargain.

Guadalupe Mountains National Park is an extraordinay land, its interrelated geology and ecology delicately balanced, but because two men and their families cared, it has been preserved.

Carlsbad Caverns National Park

I enter upon this task with a feeling of temerity as I am wholly conscious of the feebleness of my efforts to convey in words the deep conflicting emotions, the feeling of fear and awe, and the desire for an inspired understanding of the Divine Creator's work that presents to the human eye such a complex aggregate of natural wonders in such a limited space.
Robert A. Holley, 1922

A room with a ceiling twenty-five stories high and a floor of fourteen football fields – that's the Big Room of Carlsbad Caverns, the largest underground gallery of all the explored caves in the world.

One would think that this, like the attractions at Mammoth Cave in Kentucky, would have immediately appeared on the tourists lists when discovered. Not exactly. We don't know precisely when the first southwestern cowhand came across this cave, but it was in the late 1800's, too early for "tourists." Besides, Carlsbad, New Mexico, was hardly on the well-beaten track. Stages went by headed for California; but the caverns had another attraction, and beauty or fascination with geology played little part in it.

This was known as the Bat Cave at first, and that's logical. One of the things that may have sparked the first explorers was the thousands and thousands of bats that each day at sunset came fluttering out of the entrance in search of food – perhaps millions of them, since it now seems impossible to take a count. Well, where there are bats in this number, there has to be nitrate-rich guano; and there was – some fifteen thousand years of deposits.

This was the attraction at Carlsbad Caverns: bat guano. Within the twenty years just prior to its establishment as a national monument in 1923, some 100 thousand tons of guano were removed and sold as agricultural fertilizer.

In those days there *was* one man who saw something more than commercially successful business. His name was Jim White and it was Jim who, more than anyone, moved the Congress to protect this marvelous temple of underground geology. He had explored it and preached its beauty with such passion that he became its first chief ranger.

Jim White wasn't the first to see the caverns. Early Indians did not document their visits, but someone of the Basketmaker period was there. He left behind a sandal. That may have been four thousand years ago.

Carlsbad Caverns' history goes back much farther in time, perhaps 200 million years ago, when those geologic forces and seas formed the nearby Guadalupe Mountains. Like in other underground yawnings, sediments were laid, bends and cracks occurred, waters filled and drained, and minerals seeped through.

One wonders if all of these processes were as beautiful in the making as they appear today. It almost seems as if some divine decision was made to purposely seclude our geological marvels until man was ready to see and appreciate them. At any rate, it was millions of years in the making and the finished product, if indeed it is finished, carries a master's touch.

Carlsbad Caverns is beautiful. It is enormous and not yet completely explored. Seven miles of chambers and passageways are open; more exist that may lead into the Guadalupes – no one knows for certain. But those which one may visit are a wonderland of the weird; almost ghostly when specially lighted, columns standing at every turn . . . better still, they loom from the floor. Overhead hang stalactites in the shape of intricate chandeliers or frozen waterfalls; one spectacular ceiling formation is called the "Sword of Damocles." The Green Lake Room, the King's Palace, the Queen's Chambers . . . each little alcove and niche has its own special charm.

And the bat still flies. Despite the fantasyland deeper into the caverns, and the almost dread fear the little bat creates in us all, the nightly flight is one of the chief attractions here.

Would that we held this strange animal in more respect. Contrary to popular conception, this is not the vampire of fiction. Actually it is clean, timid, and a blessing in disguise. Those nightly forays into the countryside are to feed, and feed they do, on millions of beetles, moths, and other insects.

But as time passes, the bat population, like so many other things with which man tampers, is passing, too. Millions are still there, but their numbers are diminishing. You see, we are warming and drying the caverns by using the air to air-condition the park visitor center, and outside we are spreading pesticides to control the insects. One wonders . . .

It seems quite incredible to imagine the almost endless time required to form the structures such as the Giant Dome and Twin Domes in the Hall of Giants right in the Carlsbad Caverns. Each was created by droplets of water containing minute quantities of dissolved limestone which slowly formed the fantastic shapes we see today. In places the process still continues, but too slowly for us to observe during our lifetime.

In the area around and above the caverns left *and the natural entrance* right, *there are many varieties of flora, such as the claret cup cactus* above right.

Above *is the Totem Pole in the Big Room and* below *a view of the Temple of the Sun.*

Shown on these pages *is a selection from the many natural wonders in the vast, underground chambers of the Carlsbad Caverns, formed in a limestone reef by percolating ground water, beneath the rugged foothills of the Guadalupe Mountains. In this subterranean wonderland the huge galleries are filled with delicate stone formations, massive stalactites and stalagmites which, tinted by minerals in the limestone, produce a fascinating, iridescent glow.*

Petrified Forest National Park

The Forest That Was is now again the Forest That Is. But how changed!
Freeman Tilden, *The National Parks*

Economics has always been a major factor in the preservation of America's natural resources. Now more than ever we see government funding not only affect acquisitions but also the management of preserved areas. In 1892, however, it may have been an economic slump that in some ways stopped the plundering of a major national monument.

In 1858, just a few years after Arizona's great petrified forest was discovered, a German artist, Baldwin Möllhausen, accompanying a military expedition into the Southwest, published an account of what he found and, in so doing, may have opened the door for wholesale vandalism:

"We collected small specimens of all these various kinds of fossil trees, and regretted that as our means of transport were so small we had to content ourselves with fragments, which certainly showed the variety of petrification, but not the dimensions of the blocks. . . . All the way we went we saw . . . great heaps of petrifications gleaming with such splendid colors that we could not resist the temptation to alight repeatedly and break off a piece, now of crimson, now of golden yellow, and then another, glorious in many rainbow dyes."

By the 1880's, when the Atlantic and Pacific Railroad worked its way west through northern Arizona, the beauty and mysteries of trees turned to stone brought tourists by the wagonloads; and out in the same wagons when they left went bits and pieces of the forest. Like Möllhausen, they "could not resist the temptation to alight repeatedly and break off a piece."

No one really knows what was lost during the next twenty or thirty years – no one really knows how much was there to begin with – but it was staggering. Tourists sought the colorful stone for its beauty; but, more alarmingly, businesses sprung up overnight for other reasons. One South Dakota rock-polishing company took out over 400 tons of petrified wood to make mantels, tabletops, and pedestals. The marble-like stone brought outlandish prices and, no doubt, some pieces still decorate Victorian houses across America. It says something of our earliest attitudes about Petrified Forest to have had one of the first descriptions written by George Kunz, gem specialist for Tiffany's of New York.

By the 1890's vandalism had reached alarming rates. Logs were being dynamited for crystals, and in 1892 the first stamp mill was erected to grind the logs for abrasives. Commercial exploitation threatened to simply wipe the whole thing off the face of the earth, virtually before we could determine why it was there in the first place.

Then, miraculously, the bottom dropped out of the abrasive market, so to speak, and the stamp mill never turned its first wheel. There was a respite, and the concerned set about their quest for protection of this natural wonder.

It was not until 1906 that Petrified Forest National Monument was created and fifty-six more years before it attained national park status. But for the moment, at least, the vandalism was arrested. It has never really stopped. What Möllhausen began 120 years ago; a "fragment" here, a "fragment" there, is now estimated to be about twelve tons a year – twelve tons of priceless national property taken out of the park by thoughtless visitors. What is there about this petrified wood that has made it so utterly and compellingly fascinating?

The 148 square miles of land that now forms Petrified Forest National Park are like a giant jewel box. The colors of the painted desert, a portion of which is in the park boundaries, are incredibly beautiful; the silica and iron and manganese oxides of the stone trees sparkle like gems. But there is more to it than all this. There is the mystery of what Freeman Tilden called "The Forest That Was," made all the more mysterious by the mere fact that, try as one may, the eye finds absolutely no clue to the once tropical jungle of lush, exotic vegetation, lakes, and swamps, animal life unknown today, and abundant rainfall that once was here. This is the desert, and a desert it has been for millions of years. No clue at all; that is unless you look closely.

Strewn across this barren, forbidding landscape are trees – well, they look like trees; occasionally one will have roots, and on some the bark appears to have been preserved. But they are no longer upright and they are stone, stone hard enough to scratch all but the toughest of metals. Once they were giant conifers, not unlike some that still grow in South America. There were ferns and cycads and dozens of other plants. The land was flat, probably at about sea level and according to the Plate Tectonics theory, about 1,700 miles closer to the equator, and roaming around all this was a collection of giant amphibious reptiles. This was 200 million years ago in what geologists call the Late Triassic period of the Early Mesozoic era. All of these things are still there – the trees and ferns and animals . . . fossilized. The clues are in this geological graveyard if you look.

What happened? Not simple. It's as complex as the evolution of the Grand Canyon, Yosemite, or any of the other national parks. First, the trees did not fall here . . . not precisely here. Wherever they fell, they were carried here by rivers and streams that also carried great loads of sand and mud from distant

mountains. Layer upon layer of silt was piled on the trees.

Somewhere in this process great layers of volcanic ash covered everything. Water rich with silica from the ash penetrated the tissues of the pine trees, cutting off the supply of oxygen, preventing decay, and forming various kinds of quartz crystals: thus a tree that still looks like a tree but is stone.

Some of these trees, scientists think, look exactly as they did when they fell, intact and up to 160 feet in length. Others are chips and pieces as though loggers had been hard at work with axe and saw. Still others are in splinters. Within the park they are grouped in six separate concentrations: Rainbow Forest, The Long Logs, Crystal Forest, Jasper Forest, Blue Mesa, and Black Forest.

Once it was thought the supply of petrified wood was limitless, there seemed to be so much of it. It was this vast amount that prompted so much of the vandalism. This is no longer true. Geologists are certain that as time goes on erosion will uncover other trees beneath this land, as surely it will change, but the purpose of the park is to preserve what is left of this place, now, where nature gives us another kind of glimpse into the creation of the earth.

Just west of Kachina Point observation site is Chinde Point above, *from where may be seen sweeping panoramas of the Painted Desert, a strange landscape of weird shapes and a marvelous variety of colors that change* overleaf *as the direction and intensity of light changes.*

Cutting a living from this harsh land is difficult now and was no less so a thousand years ago. But there were Indians here and they left behind word that they had tried and somehow succeeded. Their petroglyphs of birds, snakes, and antelopes adorn Newspaper Rock, a seemingly aimless message so far untranslated. Occasionally a tool fashioned from petrified wood is discovered near several , long since abandoned structures. Archeological digs indicate some occupation from the Basketmaker to Pueblo periods.

At least early man seemed to find some constructive use for the ancient trees – hammerstones, points, axes, building materials. In more recent times it took the F.B.I. twenty years to track down a Phoenix man who persistently hauled away cart-loads of petrified wood to purvey to the public.

Michael Frome wrote: "I can take everything I need and want from here without removing a thing."

Arizona's Petrified Forest is unique among the petrifications of the world in its size, variety and scope. The transition from tree to stone has been so gradual and perfect that every detail, each minute fiber, is completely preserved; this, to such an extent that in some cases it is almost impossible to believe that the logs and trunks will not still feel like wood to the touch.

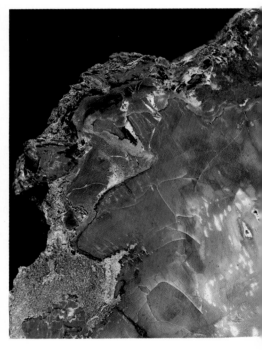

Included among the views of the park on these pages are the *Blue Mesa* above right and right *and the Painted Desert* below and bottom left. Top and top left *are shown two examples of petrified logs and* above *a close-up of one of the sections showing the beautiful, jewel-like transformation that has taken place.*

Mesa Verde National Park

It was 1280 – the year of the death of Kublai Khan, the great founder of the Mongol Empire on the other side of the earth from the Green Mesa. The people of the mesa knew nothing of Kublai Khan nor of the Mongols, though they could possibly have originated over there – sometime in the dim past perhaps having crossed the Aleutian bridge and found their way down to the tableland and canyon country where they now lived. . . .

Freeman Tilden, *The National Parks*

On December 18, 1888, two cowboys, riding through the canyons and across the mesas of southwestern Colorado looking for stray cattle, made one of the most important discoveries in North American archeology. One wishes that their motives had been less self-centered and the initial fruits of their find more scientific but, alas, like the beginnings of so many of our now protected historic areas in the United States, the story is not a pretty one.

Archeology had not come into its own as yet, but it was no deep, dark secret that early American man had established a civilization of sorts in the southwest many years before. Spanish explorers had found evidence in the 1600's, and cliff dwellings and remains of ancient campsites and villages ringed canyon walls and plateaus in the four corners area (Utah, Arizona, New Mexico, Colorado).

Richard Wetherill and Charles Mason were familiar with the Mancos Canyon country near the New Mexico border; Wetherill and his four brothers had established the Alamo Ranch near Mancos in 1879. This rugged land had already been charted by geological surveys, and Indian cliff dwellings were common sights near the ranch. But the most remarkable archeological ruins north of Mexico lay within their grasp, and for years eluded explorers and cowhands alike until that winter day in 1888.

Perhaps this is why the ruins of Mesa Verde remained untouched for so long. The land is forbidding to the traveler. Mesa Verde itself is an imposing escarpment rising 2,000 feet above the valley floor and 8,500 feet above sea level, the result of great prehistoric upheavals in the earth's crust. Even to the visitor today the approach to Mesa Verde is awesome. The huge plateaus above and to the south, however, are rich with the legacy of a lost, and, until Wetherill and Mason, forgotten culture, one of the most exciting of our national parks.

The two men who approached Cliff Palace that day were nothing short of good old American entrepreneurs. They saw the ruins for exactly what they were – a gold mine of ancient artifacts, and the following year they made their first large sale of pottery taken from Mesa Verde. Commercial exploitation continued until Mesa Verde National Park was established, and the Federal Antiquities Act was passed in 1906. Much was lost as the plundered artifacts scattered

across the country to museums and private collections and, no doubt, some to destruction.

The ancient city is quiet now; only the wind whispering through the open windows and doorways of the cliff dwellings and the scampering of wild animals across its floors give it life. At one time, as early as 500 A.D., this was a thriving community of several thousand people, struggling to exist in an inhospitable land. That they made it work is remarkable, but evidence shows they had all of the makings of a successful agricultural society.

They were short, stocky, swarthy in complexion, with black hair, high cheek bones, and slightly slanted, dark eyes, not unlike their ancestors and their descendants. No one knows how they spoke or communicated with each other; that they did, with considerable intellect, is quite evident. Their blending of agriculture, architecture, and craftsmanship into a civilization of their own astounds modern man as he overlooks this unpretentious culture that somehow slipped away.

Mesa Verde, the "green table" in Spanish, is but a small part of the Colorado Plateau, the drainage basin of the Colorado River, typified by high mesas and deep canyons. Early Americans came here some ten thousand years ago, no doubt by the frozen Aleutian link to Asia. Today man attempts to devise some pattern of life for this nomad. Although each little bone, bit of ash, and piece of carved stone offers a clue, the puzzle is still fragmented. Part lies in Mexico and Peru, part is scattered across the northern and eastern United States, and part lies here in this little corner of Colorado. To be sure, the Americans separated as they traveled south from Alaska. Some found a route farther south and established great civilizations. Some moved east and north and became the American Indian we know best and who survived the longest. Others moved to the sea and the southern California and Baja peninsula and barely existed. Those that stayed here seem to have remained for a period of about eight hundred years. Exactly why they left is the mystery that surrounds this place and has baffled archeologists for years.

That these cliff dwellers left, and left en masse, for other parts is a certainty. Their architecture suggests

Toward the end of the 12th century the Indians who lived in well made, stone houses on the mesa tops changed their way of life and moved down into the cliff-face caves these pages and overleaf. *Nobody knows exactly why they did this but it is possible that it was a defensive measure. Near the end of the 13th century these dwellings in turn were suddenly abandoned – and, again, no clear reason has emerged – leaving them very much as we see them today.*

ample protection from human enemies, so warring tribes seem remote. They were excellent farmers, however, and a long drought – narrow tree rings about the thirteenth century indicate this – or perhaps an exhausted soil that simply would not yield further existence, drove them to greener lands. Whatever the reason, the quest for survival led them elsewhere. They left no message telling us where, but throughout the tribes of the southwest, it seems certain, there is the blood of the people who once lived here – perhaps among the Hopis and other Pueblo Indians of New Mexico.

Search as we may, clues to the exodus of these people elude us, but we do not lack evidence of their life here. Spruce Tree House, for example, has been marvelously preserved. There are 114 living rooms and eight ceremonial rooms to this apartment complex, and each has offered a tiny bit of information on how the people lived and worked and played. The reconstruction of this period of our history is remarkably complete, despite the many losses, and it can be seen in graphic detail in the park museum.

Like the Inca of Peru and the Maya of Mexico – and perhaps they were really all part of the same – this civilization has vanished, leaving behind tantalizing bits and pieces of a gigantic puzzle. Sometimes we feel it is all done and there is nothing more to learn, but an archeologist's brush may yet dust off a pottery chip or an animal bone or a ceremonial trinket that will put it all together. Until then, Mesa Verde must be regarded as sacred to our American heritage. Whether or not we descend from these people, this place is a part of us.

Grand Canyon National Park

Though there are elsewhere deep canyons, some of even greater depth than the Grand Canyon, ... there is not one that can match its vastness, its majesty, its ornate sculpture and its wealth of color. Whoever stands upon the brink of the Grand Canyon beholds a spectacle unrivalled on this earth.

Francois E. Matthes,
The Grand Canyon of the Colorado River

A Texas cowboy grazing cattle in Arizona near the South Rim of the Grand Canyon suddenly found himself near the edge looking into that great chasm. He is reported to have removed his hat, wiped his brow, and said, "My God! Something has happened here!"

Hardly eloquent, that old cowhand, but search as you may for words at that first glimpse, most likely his will do. Nothing, not the camera, the canvas, or the poet, has prepared you for what may be the greatest visual shock man can experience: a pageant of time so huge and complex, so foreign to the senses, and yet so incredibly beautiful, that it is at once a frightening reality and an illusion.

J. B. Priestly wrote: "Those who have not seen it will not believe any possible description. Those who have seen it know it cannot be described."

It is best left unsaid. Preconceived notions vanish; the words of others prove inadequate; the camera fails. "My God! Something *has* happened here!"

This is not man's world. Unseen hands have created the most awesome spectacle on earth: a canyon 200 miles long, five to twelve miles wide, and 6,000 feet deep. The dimensions alone stagger the mind and, at first, turn you away. Yet, inevitably, you look back and gradually the magnificence of it all transcends that bewilderment and folds the human spirit into a glory of nature unknown before. This is the story of the earth itself, a geological calendar of time filled with the chaos of creation and the radiance of life going on. No one leaves unmoved.

When you suddenly come upon the Grand Canyon – and there is no other way, for that is the nature of the Colorado Plateau – you want to believe you are the first to see, you are the discoverer. Your eye searches and you compose; your mind sweeps the great rocks and cliffs, the gaiety of color, and soon you realize that in that brief moment it has all changed, and your words fly away. There are a thousand Grand Canyons as the sun moves across the sky, not a single minute the same as before. From the brilliance of sunrise through dazzling sunsets to the soft glow of the moon and stars, the Grand Canyon offers an infinity of moving experiences that mark the soul forever. And you are never the same.

Exploring the region in 1857, army Lieutenant Joseph Christmas Ives wrote: "It seems intended by nature that the Colorado River, along the greater portion of its lonely and majestic way, shall be forever unvisited and undisturbed." A man without vision – how wrong he was. He was not the first, of course.

Indians had lived along the rim and in the canyon itself since the twelfth century; one tribe, the Havasupai, still farms a small oasis on the canyon floor. It was their ancestors who enticed Spanish explorers into the American Southwest. López de Cárdenas and the men of Coronado's expedition saw the canyon in 1540. But they, like Ives, were unimpressed. Searching for the legendary Indian cities of gold and silver, they found the canyon only a barrier in their path. It was left to a one-armed Civil War veteran, Major John Wesley Powell, to explore the Colorado River and bring the wonders of the Grand Canyon to the world. His journals are still fresh and vibrant and still used as guides along the river.

And, of course, Ives was wrong about visitors. In 1880 an ex-miner by the name of John Hance improved the old Indian trails into the canyon from the South Rim and began leading visitors down to the river. By 1901 there were hotels and camps, and within a few years a spur of the Santa Fe Railroad to bring the unbelievers. And with them came the entrepreneurs and the conservationists.

Efforts to preserve the canyon as a national park began in 1882 shortly after the establishment of Yellowstone, when Indiana Senator Benjamin Harrison introduced legislation in the Congress. It is hard to believe now, but the bill failed, and it was not until 1893, when Harrison became President, that he was able to protect even the forest around the canyon from mining and timber prospectors. President Theodore Roosevelt in 1908 established the canyon as a national monument; by 1919 the Congress created the Grand

Canyon National Park. But its dangers were not over. As late as 1965 there were threats to build two power dams on the Colorado River that would have flooded the canyon. One dam at Bridge Canyon would have backed the river into a reservoir, within the park. After a tough battle in the Congress, the Central Arizona Project was given approval in 1968, but without the dams, and the canyon was saved.

That's how I first saw the Grand Canyon – flooded, not with water but with clouds; a sea of clouds that had drifted in the night before and covered the abyss from rim to rim, a lake of white foam. This happens from time to time, but it could not have been a more perfect introduction. The sun was just coming up and so I perched on the stone wall behind the old El Tovar Hotel and waited. Slowly the mist burned off and there . . . I felt like the Texas cowboy. *What had happened here?*

Almost every day geologists learn something new about our planet from their studies in the Grand Canyon. For nearly a century now we have pieced together an astounding story of earth erosion and upheaval spanning two billion years of the earth's existence. A century of study; that's all. A drop in the bucket of time. All we really know is that it is the Colorado River, still flowing and still carving, that has changed this land. Beyond that, it is scientific theory that we see here "nature's finest monument to the combined forces of uplift and erosion aided by an unlimited amount of time."

The Colorado begins in the Rocky Mountains and runs 1,450 miles to the Gulf of California. Along the way it is met by dozens of tributaries, the major of which is the Green River rising from the Wind River Mountains of Wyoming. Totally, the Colorado and its tributaries drain a land area of 240,000 square miles, and it drops ten thousand feet over hundreds of rapids

Bright Angel Trail below *leads from Grand Canyon Village, crossing a suspension bridge over the river, before reaching Phantom Ranch. The views from Yaki Point* above left *and* overleaf *are quite breathtaking in the immensity of scale they present.*

The Colorado River above right, *is seen from Lipan Point as it winds and twists its way through the Grand Canyon.*

before it reaches the sea.

Once, before dams were built in its path, the Colorado ran untamed, carving its way through the canyon at a speed of two to twelve miles an hour. Today its force has been subdued but still it moves more than a ton of silt each twenty-four hours, and only after this is realized can one imagine what has transpired over the years.

During the high waters of 1927, more than twenty-seven million tons of suspended solids and dissolved materials were moved in one day. This is to say nothing of the rocks and boulders that are carried across the river bed.

Despite these impressive figures, the erosion is exceedingly slow. Since man has measured, it is estimated to be about six-and-one-half inches for each one thousand years. That's a lot of centuries to just "scratch the surface" so to speak.

But is has not been the Colorado alone that has created this spectacle. There were great land upheavals, tiltings caused by pressures from beneath the earth, which caused the river to run faster and erode deeper. As it did, the sides broke away and crumbled, only to be carried away by the rushing waters. Rain and melting snow caused futher erosion, all the time cutting deeper and widening the gap.

And all of this goes on now right before the eyes. Our visits are so short, our time on earth such an infinitesimal moment on the geological calendar that we will not see any great crumbling away, but barring new earth-building events, the Colorado will go on grinding and the walls of the canyon will continue to retreat until someday, millions of years from now, only a lazy river will meander across a plain where once was this magnificent sight.

The future will be as awesome as the past, and we are only passing through as it all happens.

An evening sky softens the starkness of the vast gorge above *at Hopi Point, creating a peaceful, mystic setting. Soft colors are evident also in the views from Yaki Point* above left, *Moran Point* left, *Mohave Point* below and right *and Mather Point* overleaf.

Zion National Park

A great reservoir of the serene order of nature.
Donald Culross Peattie

When man clashes with nature, he leaves his mark. His creativity and destruction stand for centuries and, while ultimately it may be subdued, it may never be erased. Each movement he makes is telling, and those who follow with instruments to measure this and that soon put together a story of human interference in the ways of nature.

There is one thing man leaves behind that in many ways is revealing and, irrespective of the intrusion, offers something the instruments can never detect. The mark he makes on a map or the name he gives a place or thing can often tell more of the powerful struggle, the emotions, the pain and sorrow, and the joys and ecstacies of his discoveries than any computer yet devised. Such is the case in the vast country of Zion National Park, where the Mormon pioneers, seeking their ecclesiastical haven, found a certain peace and serenity. While their names for cliffs and domes and rugged canyons seem totally incongruous with the dramatic and massive forces of nature that created this place, the names stuck, and today we cannot help but agree with these people who articulated a vision. Zion itself means "the heavenly city of God." "Angel's Landing" and the "Great White Throne" at first glance look like anything but something God would have sanctioned, but this is what they saw, and who are we to dispute these temples, altars, and pulpits?

Zion is a land of "peace and comfort," as they said, but to the solely geological eye, it takes some time to piece together this handiwork of nature and find that kind of solitude. The past was less than harmonious. The elements clashed with the earth, as indeed they do still. Monolith after monolith in this park stand as mute testimony to millions of years of erosion typical of southern Utah: fierce rivers and winds that wore away sandstone during the age of dinosaurs . . . and since.

Jedediah Smith, intrepid explorer and trapper, named the river that cuts through this canyon at Zion after his friend and contemporary, Thomas Virgin. It is the Virgin, which has its origins near Bryce Canyon and joins the Colorado at Lake Mead, that has ground out much of this semi-desert wilderness. Placid at times, it can rage during replenishing torrential rains, and when it does, its force against rock is incredible; three million tons a year is moved out of Zion and on to the Colorado.

One of the Virgin's tributaries, Pine Creek, is a potent example of what has happened at Zion. When the Zion-Mt. Carmel Road was tunneled through Bridge Mountain, six windows were cut into the mountain face for view-points along the highway. The debris – one can imagine the tons of rock – was thrown into Pine Creek basin below. Within a few months

The sun flashes between the peaks above right *that form the Temples and Towers of the Virgin.*

Right *is shown the huge bulk of The Sentinel across the waters of the North Fork of Virgin River, while* above *is one of the many fascinating examples of crossbedded sandstone in the park.*

flash floods from summer rains roared through Pine Creek with mighty force and completely ground the rubble and carried it on downstream. One wonders how much of this can man-made Lake Mead handle before that body of water becomes a shallow pond. No one seems to be worried!

Zion's architecture is Navajo sandstone: sand dunes built on a desert plain for millions of years, slowly cemented in layers, and then washed and crumbled away. The colors are nothing short of a pageant, all tints and shades of red, changing with the light, seldom the same from moment to moment.

Indians lived here too, as in Canyonlands, Arches, and all the other marvelous Utah and Arizona parks, but their time had passed long before Joseph Black, Mormon pioneer, settled along the canyon's outer edge. *He* named it "Zion." Brigham Young admired it but said this was "*not* Zion." And for years it was called "Not Zion Canyon."

John Wesley Powell, on his 1872 expedition, named the north fork of the Virgin canyon "Munkuntuweap" and the east fork canyon "Parunuweap," age-old Indian designations. But Joseph Black's vision prevailed. Zion became a national monument in 1909 and later, as its boundaries were expanded in 1937 and 1957, a national park.

Zion Canyon, in Zion National Park, is a spectacular, multicolored gorge, where gigantic stone masses such as The Watchman top left and overleaf, Lady Mountain center left, The Towers of the Virgin bottom left, The Sentinel below, The Court of the Patriarchs above and The East Temple right dominate the landscape in Utah's dramatic desert and canyon country.

As a pleasing contrast to, and respite from, the great stone masses of the park, it also contains a considerable variety of plant life, much of which produces beautiful blooms in the appropriate seasons. In particular, the side canyons offer shade and moisture in which species thrive.

Left *are the flowers of the snakeweed, a member of the sunflower family;* top and below *delicate, golden columbine;* above *the leafy aster, another member of the sunflower family;* top right *the impressive bloom of the beavertail cactus;* center right *Coulter's globemallow and* bottom right, *this time a member of the mustard family, the watercress.*

Bryce Canyon National Park

Unka-timpe-wa-wince-pock-ich. *Paiute for "Red rocks standing like men in a bowl-shaped canyon."*

Bryce Canyon is changing. No, it's not disappearing; there's no need to rush. All our parks are changing in one fashion or another; such is the evolution of nature. Man has preserved them "in perpetuity," but at Bryce, where the rock formations are perhaps more delicate than at most others, the erosion is significantly pronounced. Protected forever from the ravages of the human, nature's processes continue. The towering pinnacles, those bright red and pink spires that have made Bryce Canyon so famous and popular, erode so easily and so rapidly that occasionally they crack and crumble or even collapse right before our eyes. In 1964 one of the favorite formations in the park, the arch at Oastler's Castle, collapsed as visitors looked on; one rock slide closed two of the "windows" along the Zion-Mt. Carmel tunnel. Geologists predict that the rim of the Amphitheater is receding at the rate of one foot in 50 years.

Now before you run to the calculator, that means that if you are fortunate enough to spend five or six days there, the rim of the Amphitheater may be cut back about one two-hundredth of an inch. Hardly worth your time? Of course it is; not to wait for a tumbling boulder or a slide of pebbles – it will be your lifetime, plus many others, before there is a change in the scenery, but the joy of Bryce Canyon is the breath-taking kaleidoscope of shapes and colors that dazzle the eye and mind.

The earliest white explorers and settlers who happened across much of our special scenery of the West were masters of the understatement. They were not poets or painters – these men and women did not come along until much later. They were trappers and traders and hunters and families seeking to carve out of these desolate places a bit of farm land, a plot of ground from which to draw a living. It is not so unusual, then, that their first revelations leave one generation, so fraught with show-business and political-type jargon, totally disappointed. Didn't they see what we see? To Ebenezer Bryce, Scottish emigrant and Mormon convert, who staked a claim and grazed his cattle here in the late 1870's, the canyon was simply "a hell of a place to lose a cow!"

Like his counterparts at Grand Canyon and Yosemite, Bryce found little pause in the spectacular, but he left his name behind. If he ever stood on the rim or walked the Indian trails beneath and saw any more than his cows, he never told us.

Bryce wasn't the first here, of course. There were Indians; the evidence is thin and very little is known about them. We do know that Paiutes lived in the area in more recent times, for they left something of their impressions. As so frequently happened, the Indian was more poetic than the white man. For the spires in

the amphitheater he gave us *unka-timpe-wa-wince-pock-ich*, "red rocks standing like men in a bowl-shaped canyon."

That statement rings of superstition, and no doubt it's origins are in the legend that the Indian's ancestors were sinful folk who had defied the gods and were turned to stone. All of this seems to be supported by the lack of visible signs that Indians ever ventured among their "forebears".

The Spanish were in southern Utah in 1776, but it was the Mormons, nearly a century later, who first settled the Bryce area. Their pioneer communities sprang up all around this canyon, each digging some miraculous existence from the wilderness. It was probably not until sometime later that anyone really took stock in what Ebenezer Bryce had found.

It was nearly forty years before word began to trickle out. In 1916 an article appeared in a railroad magazine, and it wasn't long before tourists began to arrive. By 1923 the boundaries of Bryce Canyon National Monument had been set; it was doubled in 1928 and established as a national park.

Bryce Canyon is not really a canyon at all. Unlike nearby Zion, which is the canyon of the Virgin River,

Bryce is the side of a plateau of varying kinds of stone that simply melted or washed away. Almost exclusively, water has been the erosive agent at Bryce, water in the form of heavy rains and snow and ice. It is more a washing process than cutting or carving as in the Grand Canyon.

There seems to have been some uplifting and tilting going on here in Utah millions of years ago, leaving great plateaus that form a natural staircase, so to speak, from Bryce southwest to the Grand Canyon. These plateaus, separated by the mighty forces of rivers, are all different in composition, and it is that composition, layer upon layer of sediment deposited when this land was all part of a great inland sea, that not only gave them their colors and names, but determined the erosion aftermath. There are the Chocolate Cliffs of Arizona at the Grand Canyon; working north are the Vermilion Cliffs, then the White Cliffs, the Gray Cliffs, and at Bryce, the Pink Cliffs. The brilliant Pink Cliffs are about 54 million years old and about 9,000 feet above sea level. The Kaibab limestone of the Grand Canyon is 225 million years old and about 2,500 feet above sea level.

The rock formations in all of these great chasms are initially dependent on the kind of sediment laid down. Fresh water lakes covered the Bryce area leaving a very fine-grained and soft siltstone and a slightly harder limestone. Sprinkled throughout are thin layers of shale. All of these erode at a different rate, thus the

The colorful, and quite incredible formations in Bryce Canyon are the result of rocks, shale and sandstones which have all eroded at different rates, allowing the elements to create fantastic sculptures and free-standing columns. Above left and overleaf *is shown Paria View;* below *Ponderosa Canyon and* above right *the aptly-named Wall of Windows, with horseback riders on Peek-a-Boo Trail in the foreground.*

variety of shapes and sizes of formations.

What entices the eye most at Bryce Canyon is, of course, the color. Iron, in the form of iron oxides, mixed with varying concentrations of manganese and copper, is responsible. The more iron, the more pink and red; the more manganese and copper, the more lavender and green. The white formations have simply had the iron leached from them.

Bryce Canyon is really two parks: the high, forested plateau and the beautiful scenery below. While the shapes and colors of the forest are entrancing in themselves, it is the view below that captures the imagination. No photograph or book prepares you for what you see, but the names give you a hint. The first overlook, just inside the main park entrance, is called "Fairyland View". That almost says it all. "Tower Bridge", "Chinese Wall", "Crescent Castle", "Sinking Ship", "Queen Victoria"—these are just a few of the intricate forms that set you off on what could be days of wandering in a fantasy land.

Someday the spires and arches will fall and the colors will change, but new ones will appear as the eroding waters seek their way to the seas: new domes and temples, some as delicate as needles, others as colossal as mountains, all molded by nature and untouched by human hand.

The Natural Bridge top right *consists of an outcrop of rock with the soft, central section worn away leaving a hole over fifty feet wide and almost twice as high. As the formation does not straddle water it could perhaps more properly be termed an arch.*

Everywhere in Bryce there are formations that seem more the products of fantasy than of nature. Center right *is Balanced Rock, and the structure* bottom right *is in Agua Canyon.* Above *is pictured the outlook from Rainbow Point;* left *looking down Navajo Loop from Sunset Point, and* below *and overleaf scenes on the Fairyland Trail.*

Arches National Park and Canyonlands National Park

It is a lovely and terrible wilderness...harshly and beautifully colored, broken and worn until its bones are exposed, its great sky without a smudge or taint from Technocracy, and in hidden corners and pockets under its cliffs the sudden poetry of springs.

Wallace Stegner, *The Sound of Mountain Water*

Utah, Arizona, New Mexico, Colorado. Four Corners. The Colorado Plateau. The land of canyons.

The Colorado Plateau is an island of flat-lying rock between the Rocky Mountains and the deserts of the West: a high, flat table, dotted here and there with isolated snow-capped peaks and laced with an interconnecting, rugged and dramatic scenery that sweeps the mind with shapes and colors. This is nature's hideaway, seemingly forbidden to man and beast alike. Water created this plateau, and it is water that has eaten into its heart and slowly, inexorably taken it away. Nowhere is this erosion more dramatically demonstrated than in the southeast corner of Utah at Arches and Canyonlands National Parks.

The mighty Colorado River, flowing from the east, meets its tributary, the Green River, flowing from the north, in the heart of Canyonlands National Park. Together they shape, as they have done longer than man knows, the most incredible examples of water erosion on the earth; there's nothing like it anywhere. And it is a monstrous task to describe. "I would describe Canyonlands as the place where the adjective died from exhaustion", wrote Freeman Tilden. He was right. Even those who attempted to name the formations relied on the noun: Bagpipe Butte, Elephant Canyon, Devil's Lane, The Sewing Machine, The Doll House. There are arches, pillars, needles, spires, pinnacles, domes, steeples, and hundreds of others that need only the eye and a vivid imagination. Massive sandstone columns stand like skyscrapers. Angel Arch has an opening 190 feet high under which could sit the Arc de Triomphe, with some 16 feet to spare. And some of this is still unexplored. What great sights await those hardy souls who will venture beyond the trails!

The scenery in Arches National Park, just to the north of Moab and only a short distance from Canyonlands, is every bit as spectacular. This small park – small in comparison to Canyonlands, but huge in its array of geological formations – lies on the north bank of the Colorado River as it passes into Utah. Here is a phenomenal collection of natural arches, windows, spires, rocks balanced precariously on rocks – the most concentrated assemblage in the country.

This park takes it name from the dominant feature, natural stone arches so delicately formed that one marvels at their stability, fearing to walk beneath lest they crack and crumble. Landscape Arch is the longest

A foothold has been gained by many varieties of plant life in this remarkable southeast corner of Utah.

Above is the Indian paintbrush, of the figwort family, and on the opposite page bottom left and above right the flowers of the western peppergrass, a member of the mustard family, soften the outlines of a gnarled and weathered tree, while far right, bottom the same plant blooms in profusion against the background of The Wooden Shoe.

in the world; it spans 291 feet and at one point is only six feet thick. No engineer could successfully duplicate it, yet nature in its infinite wisdom has been master architect.

Ninety similar arches have been found in this red-rock country and, no doubt, others have escaped the eye. This is sandstone – sand deposited 150 million years ago, hardened, and then slowly eroded away. The winds and rains and flash floods still work arranging and rearranging and, as in its neighboring park to the south, someday it will all change. Landscape Arch – that little six-foot section – will have worn away. Others will form and they, too, will dissolve until finally the tiny grains of sand, transported to distant places, will reassemble in some other shape and in some other place.

Geology dominates the landscape; it dominates life. There is little water and only sparse vegetation. Hardy junipers and pinyon pine grow in the bottomlands seeking moisture wherever it can be found. The country is desolate and as inhospitable as any in the West.

Man has simply never been able to gain a foothold in canyon country – the white man that is. The Anasazi were here and for probably a thousand years or so throughout all this land they hunted and farmed and made their pottery and baskets. How they survived we can only surmise; for their pictographs and petroglyphs, found all over the walls of Canyonlands, remain mute – intriguing and challenging, but mute. We don't even know, for example, why they left storehouses of corn, now dried stone-hard after a century of sun.

Butch Cassidy "hid out" here. Zane Grey wrote about it. John Wesley Powell put it on the map. But when it came to setting it aside as a national monument, there were those who thought "some people may be repelled and call the scenery ugly, not because it is drab or dull, but because it is so different as to be incomprehensible to them and therefore hostile".

"I cannot conceive of a more worthless and impracticable region than the one we now find ourselves in", wrote an early military explorer of the Canyonlands. He was searching for riches, and he found little of benefit in these canyons. Of course, he did not have a Geiger counter as did his twentieth-century counterpart, whose quest for uranium has left scars never to be erased. That was before 1964 and Canyonlands National Park.

But even in the park planning days, when the dedicated saw some 800 thousand acres of federally-owned land available, only 257 thousand were set aside. The governor of Utah "made it clear from the start" that he did not want park land to "lock up" resources, whatever they might be, and "damage his state's future economy."

Freeman Tilden, that grand old philosopher who was adopted by the National Park Service in 1941 and at whose feet so many of us have sat...that marvelous thinker, who died in 1980 at the age of 96, and to whom this book is dedicated...Freeman wrote in one of his most inspirational moments:

"I think America will have come to maturity when it will be possible to erect somewhere – probably it will be west of the Mississippi – a great bronze marker which will read:

Beneath these lands which surround you there lies enormous mineral wealth. However, it is the judgement of the American people, who locked up this area, that these lands shall not be disturbed, because we wish posterity to know that somewhere in our country, in gratitude to nature, there was at least one material resource that we could let alone."

137

Salt Creek drains a large part of The Needles district of Canyonlands, making its way into the Colorado River just northeast of that river's meeting with the Green River. Over an immense period of time Salt Creek has carved its way through the rock in this southern area of the park to create the impressive sights shown on these pages.

Overleaf is pictured the area known as Chesler Park, with The Needles across the background.

The yellow and gold of sunset silhouettes features of Canyonlands National Park.

Above *are the North and South Six-shooter Peaks;* center right *Island in the Sky, and from Big Spring Canyong Overlook figures* left *lend scale to the huge rock formations.*

Top right *is shown the entrance to Joint Trail, leading to Chester Park, and The Flats* below, *near Canyon Overlook.*

The fascinating petroglyhs bottom right *have been carved in the blackened surface of Newspaper Rock to reveal the clean sandstone underneath, probably over a period covering 1,000 years.*

The views right and bottom left *from the Grand View Point of Island in the Sky, in the north of Canyonlands National Park, and the Colorado River from the Colorado River Overlook* below right, *give some idea of the vast scale of this geological wonder of the Colorado Plateau.*

In spite of its name, the Devil's Kitchen above *is a surprisingly beautiful spot equipped with picnic tables, and from here the road leads into Devil's Lane toward SOB Hill* top left.

The scene center left *shows Squaw Flat, in the Needles district, while bottom is Angel Arch, at the end of Salt Creek Trail.*

Late afternoon sun emphasizes the glowing colors of the rock above *on the trail near Peekaboo Spring.*

Arches National Park lies in the heart of the famous red rock country of Utah and contains more natural stone arches, windows, spires and pinnacles than anywhere else in the country.

The formation top left is North Window, with Turret Arch in the background; top, behind the twisted tree trunk, is South Window; center left The Devil's Garden; above Upper Fiery Furnace; bottom left The Garden of Eden; below, behind the brightly colored flowers, The Organ; above right South Park Avenue and right the majestic Double Arch, while overleaf is the lovely silhouette of Delicate Arch.

Sequoia National Park and Kings Canyon National Park

Wellingtonia gigantea! Washingtonia gigantea!
Sequoia gigantea!

Wellingtonia gigantea! They almost named it that. The British, who at first believed the big tree to be a hoax – they saw only specimens and read descriptions – gave it the name *Wellingtonia gigantea.* The Americans were furious. They had discovered it, it was theirs, and no Englishman was going to name it. Dr. Jacob Bigelow, botanist with the Pacific Survey party of 1853, stepped in. "Well, let England have the empty name. *We* have the tree!" Wellington, indeed! *"Washingtonia gigantea,"* he countered.

Hungarian botanist Stephen Endlicher moderated. Neither Wellington nor Washington. Endlicher was also a linguist. It would be *Sequoia gigantea:* "Sequoia," honoring the great American Cherokee chief who created an alphabet for his people and taught them to read and write.

Somehow it fits. Besides, how could we have lived with a native tree, bearing the generic title of a British Duke, popularly called the General Grant, General Sherman, and General Lee?

But, alas, the pride in this unique bit of "American heritage" was shortlived. No sooner had that trans-Atlantic squabble been settled than promoters stripped one of the saintly Sequoias of its cinnamon-red bark, sectioned its shell, and sent the pieces off to the Crystal Palace in London for a "shilling a show." Only a handful of Americans protested this "cruel idea" and "perfect desecration." We had searched nearly a century for some cultural identity in our natural wonders and just as we were discovering and understanding the treasures we owned, an uncaring and systematic destruction began.

The first known white man to see the Sequoia here was Hale Tharp, a cattleman seeking new grazing land in 1858. Indians led him to the great meadows of the Sierras to see what they had known for centuries. Within four years the loggers had followed. Between 1862 and 1900 one of the largest and finest forests in the world – all Sequoias – was wiped out, completely. This wanton destruction included at least two trees – perhaps three or four more – that were *bigger* than today's world's largest, the General Sherman in Sequoia National Park's Giant Grove.

The Sequoia – Giant Sequoia, Sierra redwood, *Sequoiadendron giganteum* – it makes little difference; it's still the big tree. It is "a species of the genus," which is another way of saying that it's in a class by itself, the largest living thing on earth. There are cousins, the taller, coastal redwoods, and the Douglas firs soar higher, but for sheer volume the Sequoia is one of a kind. For example, the General Sherman, discovered

in 1879 by trapper James Wolverton and named for his Civil War commander, is estimated to be 2.5 thousand years old and may well be older. It is 272 feet tall – more than 100 feet higher than Niagara falls – and has a trunk diameter of 36 feet. And if that's not enough, its first limb, which just recently fell, was 130 feet from the ground and measured 7 feet in diameter.

A thousand years before Christ, when Pharaohs ruled the most civilized nation on earth, tiny seeds from no one knows where took root in America's Sierra Nevadas. Not fire, storm, nor earthquake disturbed them. They grew and grew until one could provide enough lumber for forty, five-room houses, so great was its mass. And many of them did. No one counted the big trees when they first began clearing, but between the Forest Service, the National Park Service, and the State of California, about forty thousand have been saved. Think how many fell to the loggers' saw!

The one most responsible for Sequoia National Park was John Muir, an enormously energetic man whose passion for the Sierra Nevada put much of this land into the protective custody of state and federal governments. His love for the big trees – he would often shinny up a 100-foot pine just to listen to the wind singing through the needles – saved them, and just in the nick of time. He first saw them in 1875. President Benjamin Harrison signed the legislation creating the park fifteen years later on September 25, 1890: 252 square miles, enlarged 36 years later to 604 square miles. It was our second national park.

There is nothing small about this ever-changing country. The distance from the peak of Spanish Mountain to the Kings River is greater than from the Grand Canyon rim to the Colorado. And each year it changes a little: the river grinds a little deeper, the mountains are worn down ever so slightly, the trees grow a little taller. And all of this will continue long after this civilization has vanished and until the landscape no longer resembles what we now see.

Across the top of this giant, tilted block of granite – the Sierra high country – runs the Pacific Crest Trail, which has its origins in Mexico and Canada. Here, beginning in Yosemite National Park to the north and running 225 miles south into Sequoia-Kings, it is known as the John Muir Trail, a magnificent tribute to the man who walked these mountains and who made these parks possible. The trail ends at Whitney Portal, within the shadow of Mount Whitney, the highest mountain in the conterminous United States, some fourteen thousand feet.

The valleys below are covered with ponderosa pine and white fir, the peaks above with last winter's snow. In between, deer, bobcats, and bear, and the king of trees, are in command. There are two parks here – their names are man-made boundaries – but this is truly one magnificent park, one which man once scarred, but one in which he now walks gently.

Channel Islands National Park

Until March 5, 1980, this was Channel Island National Monument and included Anacapa, Santa Barbara, and San Miguel Islands in the Santa Barbara Channel, off the coast of southern California. Now it is our fortieth and newest national park and embraces two additional islands: Santa Rosa and Santa Cruz. The first three islands were brought into the National Park Service in 1938 and have been predominately wildlife refuges since. The two new acquisitions are relatively unspoiled and will be managed as havens of a somewhat fragile ecological system. They all belong to the people now, however, and will serve as a pleasant refuge for one to become reacquainted with the sea and its environment.

Park entrance sign left *on highway 198, above the Ash Mountain Entrance Station.*

A stone stairway leads to the summit of Moro Rock below, *from where may be seen a magnificent panorama of the High Sierra.*

Above *is shown a stretch of the East Fork of the Kaweah River and* below *is the distinctive yellow flower, black-eyed Susan.*

The giant sequoia stands today as the survivor of an ancient lineage of huge trees. To touch these living giants can be, to many people, a deeply-charged emotional experience.

The Round Meadow right and below left, *the Parker Group* above left *and the Lost Grove* bottom *are all in the Giant Forest.*

Amid the spectacular giant sequoias above, with their distinctive cinnamon-colored bark, the cute ground squirrel below makes his home. Here, in Kings Canyon's Grant Grove, towers the Nation's designated Christmas Tree – the 267.4 feet General Grant left.

Shown left is the fire-ravaged trunk of Burnt Monarch; top right the gnarled stump of a giant sequoia in Big Stump Basin bottom right; center right Spring Tree which fell in 1931, in Grant Grove, and below Resurrection Tree on Big Stump Nature Trail.

Amid Yosemite's grandiose mountains and groves of conifers, tumble the crystal clear waterfalls *left that more than anything else seem to supply the exhilarating atmosphere of the "Incomparable Valley".*

In spectacular leaps the Upper and Lower Yosemite Falls above right *course down the vertical rocks that rise dramatically from the valley floor, while beyond the Merced River the mighty bulk of El Capitan faces Cathedral Rocks and the shiny ribbon of Bridalveil Fall* right.

Atop Sentinel Dome, the gnarled and twisted Jeffrey pine below *is seen in sharp relief* above *in day's final burst of sunlight.*

Southeast of Lassen Peak lies lush Kings Creek Meadows where the crystal water of Kings Creek snakes tortuously bottom *to cascade down gigantic stair-steps in the sparkling falls* left and right.

Part of Lassen's fascinating Bumpass Hell, with its self-guiding nature trail and diversified hydrothermal area, is shown top; above *Manzanita Lake, and* below left *Raker Peak, formerly Divide Peak, which was re-named in 1933 in honor of Representative John E. Raker of California.*

In contrast to Lassen's ragged volcanic landscapes are dense green forests and tranquil lakes such as *Cold Boiling Lake* top left and right; *Manzanita Lake* bottom left *and shown in winter's grip* center left *with snow-capped Lassen Peak; Hat Lake* right, *and Reflection Lake with Chaos Crags* below, *that mark the tremendous diversity of this spell-binding park.*

Hawaii Volcanoes National Park and Haleakala National Park

This was the restless surge of the universe, the violence of birth, the cold tearing away of death; and yet how promising was this interplay of forces as an island struggled to be born, vanishing in agony, then soaring aloft in triumph.

James Michener, *Hawaii*

Man believes he is on the brink of discovering the origins of life, and with the rapid advances of science and technology during the past decades, he may well be approaching something like that. Converts to the "big bang" theory of earth's creation grow steadily. To listen to the new voices of science, those like Carl Sagan who have made their theories so palatable and popular, is to believe that we can still hear the echoes of the explosion which sent this planet hurtling into space.

But what about that time between the "bang" and when life first appeared; that period of building and forming that gave us what we now see in our national parks? So little is known of the earth's history that by comparison that which eludes man's knowledge and escapes his theories, is staggering. Yet here in the Hawaiian chain of Pacific islands a new piece of the puzzle unfolds almost every day. Here the earth continues to move, to change, to reshape itself, to reveal its deep, dark, secret past, and man, that inquisitive creature who pokes and demands, sits by – a silent witness.

Hawaii is a living laboratory, one of the few places in the world where the layman, side-by-side with the scientist, watches and shares in the knowledge that all is not yet done. Steam breaks from tiny crevices in the rock, volcanic fire surges into the air from active vents, molten lava streaks down mountain flanks, and the earth trembles and thunders as the island interior moves, settles, and moves again in a constant process of building and reshaping.

Hawaii, the largest of the eight major islands in the chain, is almost hypnotic in its serenity and beauty – lush vegetation, incredibly picturesque waterfalls and shorelines, quiet, unencumbered atmosphere and lifestyle, and ideal climate. Its two, sometimes snow-capped, mountains, Mauna Loa and Mauna Kea, give the island a majesty at once separating the barren desert side from the blue-green tropical side, and completing a world ecology system in miniature.

Hanging over all of this – or, perhaps, it is better to say quietly simmering beneath – is an awesome force of pent-up energy that man cannot, and makes no attempt to, reckon with. He watches, measures, readjusts his theories, and learns. And the visitor to Hawaii Volcanoes National Park witnesses the most spectacular of nature's forces.

Unlike the Grand Canyon, where the Colorado's erosion is so infinitesimal that it can only be measured

The visible rim of Halemaumau Crater in Hawaii Volcanoes National Park can be seen above, *and* overleaf *the intricate formations of a typical pahoehoe lava field.*

in hundreds of years, the island of Hawaii grows virtually before your eyes. The last eruption, as of this writing – and they are so frequent it must be written so – was small in comparison to others in the past, but even it brought to the surface of the Kilauea caldera thousands of feet of new lava, the stuff from which this island was made.

Man has seen the birth of an island, but not here in the Pacific. At 8 o'clock on the morning of November 14, 1963, the tip of an underwater volcanic mountain began emerging from the sea, six miles off Iceland, in a series of violent explosions that sent lava and ash hundreds of feet into the air. Nearly three years later, by August 1966, the island of Surtsey had firmly planted its roots and established a named position on world maps. No one knows how far beneath the sea this mountain had been or for how long it had steadily built its way to the surface. It just happened, and, amazingly, man saw it virtually from the first explosion.

By the geological clock Surtsey was born in a matter of seconds. Someday, perhaps thousands of years from now, it will link with Iceland or itself become a major land mass. On the other hand, the sea could, by constant erosion, slowly reclaim Surtsey as it did a small islet that formed from the same eruption only yards away; visible only long enough to be named "Helmsey," it quickly disappeared.

Man has witnessed the eruptions of volcanoes, some old, some new, since recorded time; volcanoes that have destroyed civilizations and reshaped the earth. As recently as 1979 scientists found fissures on the Pacific Ocean floor, 210 miles off the Galapagos Islands, from which spewed molten magma spreading across the Mid-Oceanic Ridge of undersea mountains.

But what scientists saw near Iceland, and are now seeing along the Galapagos rift, is what they missed in the mid-Pacific; the birth of an island that one day would be the focal point for their study of volcanism. The island of Hawaii began much the same way as Surtsey and perhaps from now-familiar fissures in the ocean floor, some two to three million years ago. Its peaks may not have broken the sea's surface until 500,000 years ago, no doubt after man walked upright in the Olduvai Gorge of Africa. The island of Hawaii, then, is young by comparison to the others in this chain. They have long since passed over the hot spot in the earth's mantle and will never erupt again.

Let's pause for a moment, for that last statement, when thoroughly digested, can be as startling as the scientific theory behind it.

The Hawaiian Islands are one of the best illustrations of "plate tectonics" on the globe, and it's not all that difficult to understand. The earth's crust is made up of a number of sections or plates that move about as though they were gliding over the mantle beneath. The Pacific plate is one of those and the Hawaiian Islands are right in the middle. The plate is moving, imperceptibly, of course, toward the northwest, and taking the islands with it. Somewhere beneath all of this is a "hot spot," a vent through which molten lava is forced to the earth's surface by internal pressures of incredible magnitude. At one time the mountains and islands to the northwest were directly over this vent – Kohala at the northwest end of the island, Haleakala on Maui, and so on – now Hawaii is there and we can literally see the progression of volcanic life and death.

Each of these islands, when over the hot spot, were formed of the lava forced to the surface. As the plate moved on, about three to five inches a year, the volcanoes were severed from their earth-building source and died. Life erupted again, over that same vent in the mantle, a few million years later and a few miles to the southeast. At this rate, in 12,672 years, it may be estimated, Hawaii will be one mile to the northwest. In three to five million years it will be about where Honolulu is now, and . . . it staggers one's thinking, this plate tectonics, for, far into the future, some seventy million years from now, Hawaii will reach the edge of the Pacific plate near where the Aleutian Islands are now, where it will meet the Asian plate and be folded back into the mantle from which it came. Meanwhile, back in the Pacific, new paradises will have risen from the ocean floor, just as these beautiful islands did, and the earth's evolution will go on as before.

Of the five volcanoes on Hawaii, Kohala at the northwest end of the island is the oldest. It has not erupted in historic times and clearly shows what erosion can do without the constant lava regeneration. Hualalai, above Kailua, Kona, last erupted, geologists think, in 1850. Mauna Kea, the highest peak on the islands, has slept for more than 4,500 years. The two remaining, Mauna Loa and Kilauea, are among the most active volcanoes in the world. Mauna Loa erupted briefly in 1975, covering a five square mile area with lava. Kilauea has erupted every year, except two, since 1959 and in that twenty-one year period has added nearly one billion cubic yards of lava to the island.

The two volcanoes are a part of Hawaii Volcanoes National Park, one of the most beautiful and, without doubt, the most exciting park in the system. National park status is synonymous with protection and preservation and one immediately wonders why it is necessary to provide these services to an area so geologically active, where man dare not tamper with nature. The truth is that all of the Hawaiian Islands have been altered so markedly by man, especially the Caucasians, that when understood in the overall context of things, the wonder is why the entire chain is not one huge park.

The most important thing is that both civilizations, the native who arrived about 1,200 years ago, and the white man who came in 1778, have held Hawaii's volcanoes in highest esteem. To the native these mountains have become an intricate part of religious fundamentals. The white man regards them as places of unusual beauty and scientific importance. Together both cultures stand in awe.

Off to the northwest, and within sight of Hawaii, is Maui, one of the youngest islands in the chain, and, assuming the islands are indeed moving in that direction, the last island to have major volcanic activity. Maui began as two volcanoes which, after many eruptions and lava flows, were eventually joined by a bridge of land between them. The largest of the two mountains is Haleakala, "House of the Sun," twelve thousand feet above sea level. This is Haleakala National Park. Last active in 1790, Haleakala is now dormant. While earthquake records indicate that there is still some adjustment taking place beneath, it is not likely ever to erupt again. But no one really knows.

Haleakala's last major activity can be dated to some one thousand years ago, but by scientific analysis on lava-covered trees on the island, other eruptions date to 9,300 years ago. Whenever, it was obviously for a sustained period and no doubt violent in every sense of the word.

The deep depression on the summit of Haleakala is often called a "crater," but in fact it is a nineteen square mile impression caused mostly by water erosion. Inside the "crater," however, can be found the cinder cones of numerous volcanic eruptions. The crater walls have been worn away by lava spills and rain erosions down

The saw-toothed Grand Teton mountain range top left, *and seen in the background of the convoluted Snake River* above *and* center left *began as a gigantic fault block uplifted from the earth's crust. Sculptured by streams and glaciers, these spectacular peaks now form a chain of pyramids, soaring more than a mile above the sagebrush flats and morainal lakes of Jackson Hole.*

The highest peak of the range, Grand Teton bottom left, *which rises to a breathtaking height of 13,747 feet above sea level, dominates the distant horizon over Snake River* below; *its jagged peaks enhanced by the tall, golden-leaved aspen trees* below right *beyond Rockefeller Parkway, and the old buckrail fence lining the Jackson Hole Highway* above right.

Some of the glaciers which gave the range its present form still remain and frigid glacial lakes dot the landscape. Of these possibly the most famous is Jenny Lake, which lies motionless at the foot of Grand Teton and Mount Teewinot overleaf.

Glacier National Park

Give a month at least to this precious reserve. The time will not be taken from the sum of your life. Instead of shortening,
it will indefinitely lengthen it and make you truly immortal.
John Muir

John Muir could have been writing about any of America's national parks, but Glacier is a very special place – some claim the most beautiful of all the parks – and it takes time to enjoy and understand, time never missed in the scheme of things. There's an old story told – told by nearly everyone who writes about Glacier, but well worth repeating – of the man who seemed disappointed that there was "nothing exciting" to do at the park. "What the hell do you expect me to do here," he asked, "look at the *scenery*?"

It is quite difficult to believe that anyone can enter Glacier and not be in awe of the mighty works of nature. Assuming that some fail to see, one can only feel sorry for those who seek more exciting things than "a look at the scenery." The towering majesty of Glacier National Park is as spectacular as any place on earth and to see is to communicate with nature. Here is truly a wonder of America, indeed of the world.

This grandeur is not all ours. We share it with Canada where the northern extension of Glacier Range in Alberta is Waterton Lake National Park. Together the two form the Waterton-Glacier International Peace Park, authorized and established in 1932 by the United States Congress and the Canadian Parliament as "a symbol of permanent peace and friendship."

The mountains of Glacier National Park are a part of the Rockies, that upheaval of mountain building that began about 75 billion years ago and extended in distance from South America through Mexico and the United States and Canada into Alaska and the Aleutians. But what we see here is much more than just mountain building; it is mountain shaping in the classical sense. The park is named for the prehistoric forces that formed it; the mighty glaciers of the ancient ice ages. And there are sixty-some within the park that still press down the mountain slopes, grinding and carving and shaping as their predecessors did eons ago.

Of course, the mountains came first. Geologists vary in their estimates of exactly when, but it makes little difference. They *are* in agreement, however, on how it all happened. After millions of years of sediment deposits, as much as thirty-five thousand feet, from a shallow body of water that covered the western United States, this land began to warp and buckle and crack, and ancient rock pushed up and through the earth's crust. Unlike the Southern, or Colorado Rockies – rather orderly they – this three hundred mile range was squeezed together in a vise-like grip that forced the rock sideways to the east in a fold called an overthrust. The geological formations that form

Glacier's east wall, and attract scientists from the world over, show that this mass was pushed some forty miles eastward. The mountains approached from the east, then, give the impression that they were pushed up right where they are. There are no foothills as there are on the western slopes. The farthest extension of this overthrust is Chief Mountain in the northeast corner of the park. Here the younger and older rock, one having overlapped the other, are quite evident.

But like all the mountains here, the Chief has been worn away and shaped by the ice ages that once covered all but the very peaks. There were four great periods of ice that worked their way through these mountains: the first beginning some three million years ago, the last about ten to twelve thousand years ago. It was these great rivers of ice flowing around the mountains that created the "Matterhorn" peaks.

The glaciers in the park today, the Grinnell, Salamander, and Sperry, are examples of what was here before. These have come only recently in time, perhaps as late as a thousand years ago, and they too

Amid the snow-filled canyons of the spectacular Cascade Range above, above right and overleaf, *the isolated peak of Mount Oberlin* right *is dramatically framed by the darkened tunnel on Logan Pass.*

are rapidly melting away. When first discovered in the late 1800's, both the Grinnell and Sperry glaciers covered areas of one thousand acres. Today they are only about three hundred acres in size. On a much smaller scale, these glaciers are doing what the others did.

At the height of the glacial periods, these valleys were filled with ice, as much as three thousand feet thick, and at least one extended forty miles into the Montana plains. The glaciers' paths can be measured by the knife-like ridges, the peaks, the passes, the valleys, and the debris left behind. Some flowed quite rapidly, that is rapidly for a glacier – several feet a day. Today's ice flows much more slowly; Grinnell has been "clocked" at about one inch a day. Nonetheless, the constant motion of the thick, plastic-like ice at the bottom, combined with the huge boulders and rocks it carries, is what has sliced the mountains and dug the valleys and basins.

Glacier is the only area south of the Canadian border with a subarctic climate, and the plant and animal life reflect that. What was here prior to the ice age, if anything, is unknown, for the glaciers virtually denuded the mountains of any fossils; but despite the deceiving, barren-like appearance of the mountains, the park is a true wilderness, an ideal setting for a wide variety of wildlife and plants.

The mountain heights capture the abundant rainfall from the Pacific coast on the western slopes producing dense forests of larch, spruce, fir, and lodgepole pine. Here the western, red cedar and hemlock reach their eastern boundaries. On the east side, where the Montana plains and the mountains meet rather abruptly, the prairie flora prevails: pasque flower, red and white geraniums, gailardia, asters, shooting star, and the Indian paintbrush. The short-lived alpine display is every bit as splendid and can be easily seen along the hundreds of miles of trails through the upper reaches of the park.

One of the joys of Glacier National Park is that the wildlife, once hunted for sport and food, is now protected. If there is such a thing as animals sensing their freedom, it is probably demonstrated best here. While the deer, elk, moose, and bear are no more friendly here than in other parks, they are abundant and for the most part visible to the visitor. If you are "looking at the scenery," seldom will you have to complain about sightings.

Man confers "official" on many things. Here he has given the distinction to the mountain goat, the "official" animal of Glacier National Park. Unpretentiously, this mammal wears its title well. Actually it is an antelope and not a goat at all, but seen scampering along the most precipitous cliffs and slickest rock formations, titles and names matter little to it or the visitor. It is a marvelous animal that astounds you and at the same time makes you envious of its agility.

Peter Fidler, a scout for the Hudson's Bay

Company in 1792, was the first white man to see the Waterton-Glacier area. He found the Piggan Indian had been here long before and, no doubt, other prehistoric Indians prior to that. Settlement was slow and tedious through the nineteenth century as rugged terrain and fierce Indian reluctance to yield territory presented barriers. The conquering of the Indian was much as in other areas of the West, and ultimately the pressures of the fur trade and mining interests forced a withdrawal and the "dudes" from the east moved in.

The Great Northern Railroad is as responsible as anything for the development of Glacier National Park. By 1891 it had laid a line across Montana and over Marias Pass to Kalispell, along the southern end of the area. Within thirty years after the railroad came, mining potential decreased dramatically. The Great Nothern, politicians, and conservationists joined hands in urging the Congress to preserve the area in its natural state. Glacier became a national park on May 11, 1910.

Nowhere is the work of glaciers quite so evident as here in Montana, a place of extraordinary beauty. It has been called the "Crown of the Continent," where the mountains unfold into a panorama of cathedral-like spires before the eyes. It was meant to be seen, to be felt, to be worshipped.

View after view within this glorious terrain reveals a sea of illimitable peaks, their muted splendor a glorious background for a myriad jewel-like lakes. Pictured above are the craggy pinnacles of Grinnel Point and Mount Gould beyond Swiftcurrent Lake; below Citadel Mountain and St. Mary Lake; right the peaks of Upper St. Mary Valley from Cut Bank; left Mount Clements, forming a perfect backdrop for a carpet of glacier lilies, and above left the famed Weeping Wall on Going to the Sun Road.

Olympic National Park

Olympic is the gift of the sea.
National Park Service

Olympic National Park is a rain forest; it is a lofty mountain, millions of years old; it is a stretch of nearly virgin Pacific coastline; it is a classic wilderness with wild rivers and streams, alpine lakes and meadows, a host of animal life, one thousand species of plants, and tall trees . . . Olympic National Park is all of these.

It begins along a fifty mile section of rugged coast where trees grow on the very edge of the Pacific Ocean and where the life-giving water cycle that *is* Olympic has its start and end. This islanded and rocky strip of beach along Washington's Pacific shore is one of the most primitive sections of seacoast yet remaining in the United States. Here is the great Olympic Rain Forest, a luxuriously green woodland that rivals any tropical jungle for beauty and wildlife – an environment unto itself where trees a thousand years old survey the world from three hundred feet and shield a carpet of dense moss and ferns.

Forty miles to the east stands Mount Olympus, highest of the Olympic mountains at 7,965 feet. The Olympics of the Coast Range are among the youngest mountains in the world – perhaps two million years old, but young by the geological clock. They rise from lush, green lowlands to gleaming snow-capped peaks and ridges on the Olympic Peninsula, an area of five thousand square miles, of which four thousand are mountainous.

This is a strange conglomeration of rock, a mixture of old and new, that has been pushed up between two crustal plates – the Juan de Fuca plate moving eastward and folding over and under the North American continental plate. Much of the top layer of these mountains then is ocean-floor sediment mixed with some volcanic rock spilled over from fissures. There are no volcanoes in this range.

Glaciers are the principal sculptors of the Olympics and fifty or sixty still work their way in, over, and around these peaks. Olympus alone has seven, the largest, the Hoh, about 3.5 miles long. The Blue Glacier is perhaps thirty feet thick, the result of the prodigious amount of snowfall Olympus receives each year – in one recent measurement as much as 450 inches.

That snowfall is one of the keys to the nature of Olympic National Park, "a gift of the sea." Clouds born over the Pacific and carried eastward on the moist sea winds, are wrung dry by the mountain range. They shed – sometimes fast and hard – their moisture on this peninsula in incredible quantity; in the coastal rain forests the precipitation is 140 inches per year. Glaciers build and melt, rivers and streams swell, the water running rapidly back to the Pacific, nurturing and sculpting as it goes. The cycle is so extreme in such a concentrated space that Mount Olympus is the wettest

spot in the entire United States, with some 200 inches of rainfall each year.

In contrast to this, the eastern side of the Olympics receives less than twenty inches of rainfall and nearly all farming in the Sequim Valley necessitates irrigation. The clouds are spent on the western slopes.

As the Atlantic clashes with the rock-bound coast of Maine, so the Pacific, unchecked for five thousand miles, pounds relentlessly – two tons per square inch, it is estimated – against Washington's shores. It builds and tears away at the same time in a never-ending contest of force and strength. The sea rises and recedes; five times the Pacific has flooded this coast. Now it is changing again. Wharves built seventy years ago are now one mile inland; beach fronts of the old days are now high and dry, presenting complex legal problems of ownership. Still the ocean bites away at islands and huge seastack formations, cracking and breaking, forming and reforming. Here, and at Acadia National Park in Maine, the forces of the sea are mighty; the Pacific and the Atlantic – mighty battering rams – powerful strengths of nature that change the earth.

The discovery of the Olympic Peninsula is a hodge-podge of nationalities and flags – Spanish, Greek, English, perhaps French, and Chinese. The first, of course, were the ancestors of the native American, that is the Mongols who crossed the Bering bridge. (This theory has been punctured somewhat in recent times,

but until more solid evidence to the contrary comes along, the Bering Strait story still holds water.)

The first seaman to sail this northern Pacific coast may have been a Buddhist monk in A.D. 499. His name was Hwui Shan and he wrote of following the Pacific rim from China, past the Aleutian Islands, and south to Mexico. He makes no mention of land between the Aleutians and Baja California, but if indeed he made such a voyage, he no doubt touched this land some place. The story is conjectural at best, but interesting to speculate at least.

Juan de Fuca, a Greek sailing under the Spanish flag in 1592, is the generally accepted discoverer. Even his stories are disputed, but there seems to have been enough substance to stick. At any rate, Juan Perez first sighted Mount Olympus in 1774 and named it Santa Rosalia. The Spanish flag had been planted.

Naturally the British disputed. Captain James Cook sailed by in 1778 and proclaimed De Fuca a fraud. From that point on, until 1795 when the British Union Jack replaced the Spanish flag, and from then to 1846 when the Stars and Stripes were raised, the Pacific northwest coast was the subject of controversy and conflict.

By 1849 settlement was underway with fur-trapping by the French-Canadians and timber-cutting by the early pioneers from the east and mid-west, but all of this only along the coast; the interior of the Washington territory was a mystery. In 1890 the Seattle *Press* financed a party of five civilians into the wilderness and for the first time Mount Olympus was on the map.

Later that year when the *Press* party returned they reported, "The interior of the Olympics is useless for all

Boating on beautiful Lake Crescent left, *swimming* above, *picnicking* below, *or a walk through the majestic Hall of Mosses in the dense Rain Forest* overleaf, *are among the many visitor activities to be enjoyed in enchanting Olympic National Park.*

practical purposes. It would, however, serve admirably for a national park."

No national park was ever created that easily, but they all began with a spark, and this was one. Olympic became a national monument in 1909. In 1938 it was enlarged and designated a national park. In 1953 the coastal area was added; now it contains in all 900 thousand acres.

"Useless for all practical purposes?" Hardly! "Serve admirably for a national park?" Indeed! There *were* some men of vision among our pioneers.

Above the ragged summits and glacier-strewn valleys center left, *gleaming Denali, as the Athabaskans called this 16,000 foot mountain, presides benignly, its massive bulk, seen from Mount Healy* above, *and reflected in the tundra pond* right, *dwarfing the shuttle bus that perches at its base* top left. *Yet the park is not solely one vast sea of shimmering peaks, for across wide areas moist tundra surrounds isolated patches of timberline spruce* below, *and brilliantly-hued alpine flowers, like the purple mountain saxifrage* bottom left, *pattern the green background during June and July.*
(Photo above: Fred Hirschmann; all other photos National Parks Service).

Within the seemingly inhospitable confines of the vast wilderness that is Mount McKinley National Park, a dazzling array of fascinating subarctic wildlife, including the captivating Arctic ground squirrel above, *boreal owl* left, *willow ptarmigan* below, *grizzly bear* right *and caribou* above right, *share their habitat in an enduring, albeit delicate, balance, for it is the harsh conditions of the winter months that obviously offer the greatest challenge. For the majority of the 149 species of birds the answer is clear – they migrate to the warmer climes of the south; animals such as the ground squirrel hibernate, while for those that remain, nature aids in the form of ingenious metabolic adaptations that can involve the exchanging of summer-tundra coats, as in the case of the snowshoe hare, whose white, winter coat blends perfectly with the landscape.* (National Park Service Photos).

National Park Guide

There are more than 300 areas in the National Park System, forty of which are designated National Parks. Many of these are in "out-of-the-way" places, but all are accessible to the public and most all provide the standard activities, facilities, and services. The following is an abbreviated guide to the forty National Parks. For a free folder that will assist in planning a visit, write to the Superintendent at each site. Interpretive publications of all kinds are sold in visitor center bookstores. For order-by-mail catalogs, write to the Cooperating Association in care of the park.

Acadia National Park
Mailing address: RFD 1, Box 1, Bar Harbor, ME 04609; *Telephone:* 207-288-3338; Location: 75.6 km (47 mi) southeast of Bangor on Maine 3; *Fees:* camping $4; *Activities:* camping, hiking, self-guiding trails, interpretive talks/walks, picnicking, fishing, swimming, horseback riding, biking, exhibits, av programs; *Facilities:* none; *Services:* first aid, publications, film.

Arches National Park
Mailing address: Canyonlands National Park, 446 South Main St., Moab, UT 84532; *Telephone:* 801-259-5267; *Location:* 8 km (5 mi) northwest of Moab on US 163; *Fees:* entrance $1, camping $3; *Activities:* camping, hiking, self-guiding trails, backcountry use, interpretive talks/walks, picnicking, exhibits, av programs; *Facilities:* none; *Services:* first aid, publications, film.

Badlands National Park
Mailing address: P.O. Box 6, Interior, SD 57750; *Telephone:* 605-433-5361; *Location:* 4.3 km (2.5 mi) east of Interior on South Dakota 377; *Fees:* entrance $1, camping $3; *Activities:* camping, hiking, self-guiding trails, backcountry use, interpretive talks/walks, picnicking, exhibits, av programs; *Facilities:* lodging (Cedar Pass Lodge, 605-433-5460), restaurant; *Services:* first aid, religious services, publications, film.

Big Bend National Park
Mailing address: Big Bend National Park, TX 79834; *Telephone:* 915-477-2251; *Location:* 660 km (410 mi) west of San Antonio via US 90 & 385; 520 km (323mi) east of El Paso via Int. 10, US 90, Texas 118; *Fees:* camping $2; *Activities:* camping, hiking, self-guiding trails, backcountry use, interpretive talks/walks, picnicking, fishing, horseback riding, exhibits, av programs; *Facilities:* lodging (Chisos Mountains Lodge, 915-477-2291), restaurant, post office; *Services:* first aid, groceries, supplies, gas, minor auto repairs, showers, laundry, publications, film.

Bryce Canyon National Park
Mailing address: Bryce Canyon, UT 84717; *Telephone:* 801-834-5322; *Location:* on Utah 12, 27.4 km (17 mi) off US 89; *Fees:* entrance $2, camping $2; *Activities:* camping, hiking, self-guiding trails, backcountry use, interpretive talks/walks, picnicking, horseback riding, cross-country skiing, snowshoeing, snowmobiling, exhibits, av programs; *Facilities:* lodging (Bryce Lodge, 702-733-2033), restaurant; *Services:* first aid, groceries, supplies, gas, religious services, publications, film.

Canyonlands National Park
Mailing address: 446 South Main St., Moab, UT 84532; *Telephone:* 801-259-7165; *Location:* Needles District, 56 km (35mi) south of Moab on US 163, 56 km (35 mi) west on Utah 211; Island in the Sky District, 16 km (10 mi) north of Moab on US 163, 42 km (26 mi) southwest on Utah 313; *Fees:* camping $2; *Activities:* camping, hiking, self-guiding trails, backcountry use, interpretive talks/walks, picnicking, horseback riding, boating, rafting, exhibits, av programs; *Facilities:* none; *Services:* first aid, publications, film.

Capitol Reef National Park
Mailing address: Torrey, UT 84775; *Telephone:* 801-425-3871; *Location:* 19 km (12 mi) east of Torrey on Utah 24; *Fees:* camping $2; *Activities:* camping, hiking, self-guiding trails, backcountry use, interpreting talks/walks, picnicking, exhibits, av programs; *Facilities:* none; *Services:* first aid, publications, film.

Carlsbad Caverns National Park
Mailing address: 3225 National Parks Highway, Carlsbad, NM 88220; *Telephone:* 505-885-8884; *Location:* 32 km (20 mi) southwest of Carlsbad, 242 km (150 mi) east of El Paso, Texas, on US 62, 180; *Fees:* entrance $3; *Activities:* hiking, backcountry use, interpretive talks/walks, cave tours, picnicking, exhibits, av programs; *Facilities:* restaurant, nursery, kennel; *Services:* first aid, publications, film.

Channel Islands National Park
Mailing address: 1699 Anchors Way Dr., Ventura, CA 93003; *Telephone:* 805-644-8157; *Location:* southbound on California 101, offramp in Ventura harbor south to Beechmont; northbound on California 101, take Victoria offramp in Ventura, follow signs; *Fees:* excursion fee to islands, $16; *Activities:* camping, hiking, self-guiding trails, picnicking, fishing, boating, snorkeling, swimming, scuba diving, exhibits, av programs; *Facilities:* none; *Services:* first aid, publications, film.

Crater Lake National Park
Mailing address: P.O. Box 7, Crater Lake, OR 97604; *Telephone:* 503-594-2211: *Location:* US 62 (south and west entrances), Oregon 138 (north entrance); *Fees:* entrance $2, camping $3; *Activities:* camping, hiking, self-guiding trails, backcountry use, interpretive talks/walks, picnicking, fishing, cross-country skiing, snowshoeing, exhibits, av programs; *Facilities:* lodging (Crater Lake Lodge, 503-594-2511), restaurant; *Services:* first aid, groceries, supplies, gas, publications, film.

Everglades National Park
Mailing address: P.O. Box 279, Homestead, FL 33030; *Telephone:* 305-247-6211; *Location:* 20 km (12 mi) southwest of Homestead on Florida 27; *Fees:* entrance $2, camping $3; *Activities:* camping, hiking, backcountry use, interpretive talks/walks, picnicking, fishing, boating, exhibits, av programs; *Facilities:* lodging (The Everglades Park Catering Co., 813-695-3101); restaurant; *Services:* first aid, groceries, supplies, gas, minor auto repairs, equipment rentals, religious services, publications, film.

Glacier National Park
Mailing address: West Glacier, MT 59936; *Telephone:* 406-888-5441; *Location:* on US 2 & 89; *Fees:* entrance $2, camping, $3; *Activities:* camping, hiking, self-guiding trails, backcountry use, interpretive talks/walks, picnicking, fishing, horseback riding, biking, boating, cross-country skiing, snowshoeing, exhibits, av programs; *Facilities:* lodging (Glacier Park Lodge, 406-226-4841); restaurant, post office; *Services:* first aid, groceries, supplies, gas, minor auto repairs, religious services, publications, film.

Grand Canyon National Park
Mailing address: P.O. Box 129, Grand Canyon, AZ 86023; *Telephone:* 602-638-2411; *Location:* South Rim, 96.6 km (60 mi) north of Williams, 92 km (57 mi) west of Cameron on Arizona 64; North Rim, 70 km (43 mi) south of Jacob Lake on Arizona 67 (North Rim closed mid-October to mid-May); *Fees:* entrance $2, camping $3; *Activities:* camping, hiking, self-guiding trails, backcountry use, interpretive talks/walks, picnicking, fishing, mule trips, biking, boating, river tours, exhibits, av programs; *Facilities:* lodging (Grand Canyon Lodges, 602-638-2401), restaurants, bank, post office; *Services:* first aid, groceries, supplies, gas, minor auto repairs, equipment rentals, religious services, publications, film.

Grand Teton National Park
Mailing address: P.O. Drawer 170, Moose, WY 83012; *Telephone:* 307-733-2880; *Location:* 21 km (13 mi) north of Jackson on US 26, 89, & 187; *Fees:* entrance $2, camping $3; *Activities:* camping, hiking, self-guiding trails, backcountry use, interpretive talks/walks, mountain climbing, picnicking, fishing, horseback riding, biking, boating, cross-country skiing, snowshoeing, snowmobiling,

exhibits, av programs; *Facilities:* lodging (Grand Teton Lodge, 307-543-2855), restaurant, post office; *Services:* first aid, groceries, supplies, gas, minor auto repairs, religious services, publications, film.

Great Smoky Mountains National Park

Mailing address: Gatlinburg, TN 37738; *Telephone:* 615-436-5615; *Location:* 3.2 km (2 mi) south of Gatlinburg on US 441; *Fees:* camping $4; *Activities:* camping, hiking, self-guiding trails, backcountry use, interpretive talks/walks, picnicking, fishing, horseback riding, biking, exhibits, av programs; *Facilities:* lodging (Wonderland Hotel, rustic, 615-436-5490; LeConte Lodge, 615-436-4473), restaurant; *Services:* first aid, religious services, publications, film.

Guadalupe Mountains National Park

Mailing address: 3225 National Parks Highway, Carlsbad, NM 88220; *Telephone:* 915-828-3385; *Location:* US 62 & 180, 88.5 km (55 mi) southwest of Carlsbad, New Mexico; 177 km (110 mi) east of El Paso, Texas; *Fees:* none; *Activities:* camping, hiking, backcountry use, interpretive talks/walks, picnicking; *Facilities:* none; *Services:* first aid, publications.

Haleakala National Park

Mailing address: P.O. Box 537, Makawao, Maui. HI 96768; *Telephone:* 808-572-9177; *Location:* 43 km (27 mi) from Kahului Airport via Hawaii 378; *Fees:* none; *Activities:* camping, hiking, backcountry use, interpretive talks/walks, picnicking, horseback riding, exhibits, av programs; *Facilities:* none; *Services:* first aid, publications, film.

Hawaii Volcanoes National Park

Mailing address: Hawaii Volcanoes National Park, HI 96718; *Telephone:* 808-967-7311; *Location:* 46 km (29 mi) southwest of Hilo on Hawaii 11; *Fees:* none; *Activities:* camping, hiking, backcountry use, interpretive talks/walks, picnicking, swimming, horseback riding, exhibits, av programs; *Facilities:* lodging (Volcano House, 808-967-7321), restaurant, post office; *Services:* first aid, publications, film.

Hot Springs National Park

Mailing address: P.O. Box 1860, Hot Springs, AR 71901; *Telephone:* 501-624-3383; *Location:* US 70, 270, & Arkansas 7; visitor center at Central and Reserve Aves.; *Fees:* camping $3; *Activities:* camping, hiking, self-guiding trails, interpretive talks/walks, bathhouse tours, picnicking, exhibits, av programs; *Facilities:* 12 bathing establishments (5 in city, 4 in park); *Services:* first aid, publications.

Isle Royale National Park

Mailing address: 87 North Ripley St., Houghton, MI 49931; *Telephone:* 906-482-3310; *Location:* island accessible only by NPS boat from Houghton, Michigan, commercial boats from Copper Harbor, Michigan, and Grand Portage, Minnesota; *Fees:* boat fees to island; *Activities:* camping, hiking, self-guiding trails, backcountry use, picnicking, fishing, interpretive talks/walks, exhibits, av programs; *Facilities:* lodging (Rock Harbor Lodge, 906-482-2890), restaurant; *Services:* first aid, some groceries, supplies, publications, film.

Kings Canyon National Park

See Sequoia-Kings Canyon National Parks.

Lassen Volcanic National Park

Mailing address: Mineral, CA 96063; *Telephone:* 916-595-4444; *Location:* California 36 & 44, east and west, 77.2 km (48 mi) east of Redding; California 89, north and south; *Fees:* entrance $1, camping $2; *Activities:* camping, hiking, self-guiding trails, backcountry use, interpretive talks/walks, picnicking, swimming, biking, downhill/cross-country skiing, exhibits, av programs; *Facilities:* lodging (Drakesbad Guest Ranch, 916-595-3306), restaurant, ski tows, boat ramps; *Services:* first aid, groceries, supplies, gas, equipment rentals, publications, film.

Mammoth Cave National Park

Mailing address: Mammoth Cave, KY 42259; *Telephone:* 502-758-2251; *Location:* 14.5 km (9 mi) northwest of Park City off Int 65, via Kentucky 255 from Park City, Kentucky 70 from Cave City; *Fees:* camping $3; *Activities:* camping, hiking, guided cave tours, interpretive talks/walks, picnicking, fishing, exhibits, av programs; *Facilities:* lodging (Mammoth Cave Hotel, 502-758-2225),

restaurant, post office; *Services:* first aid, groceries, supplies, gas, laundry, publications, film.

Mesa Verde National Park

Mailing address: Mesa Verde National Park, CO 81330; *Telephone:* 303-529-4465; *Location:* off US 160, midway between Cortez and Mancos; *Fees:* entrance $2, camping $2; *Activities:* camping, limited hiking, self-guiding trails, interpretive talks/walks, picnicking, exhibits, av programs; *Facilities:* lodging (Far View Lodge, 303-529-4421), restaurant, post office; *Services:* first aid, groceries, supplies, gas, minor auto repairs, laundry, religious services, publications, film.

Mount McKinley National Park

Mailing address: P.O. Box 9, McKinley Park, AK 99755; *Telephone:* 907-683-2294; *Location:* 386 km (240 mi) north of Anchorage, 193 km (120 mi) south of Fairbanks on Alaska 3; *Fees:* camping, free to $4; *Activities:* camping, hiking, self-guiding trails, interpretive talks/walks, fishing, cross-country skiing, exhibits, av programs; *Facilities:* lodging (McKinley Park Station Hotel, 907-683-2215), restaurant; *Services:* first aid, groceries, supplies, publications, film.

Mount Rainier National Park

Mailing address: Tahoma Woods, Star Route, Ashford, WA 98304; *Telephone:* 206-569-2211; *Location:* 113 km (70 mi) southeast of Tacoma on Washington 7 & 706, 153 km (95 mi) southeast of Seattle, 166 km (103 mi) west of Yakima; *Fees:* entrance $2, camping $3; *Activities:* camping, hiking, self-guiding trails, backcountry use, mountain climbing, interpretive talks/walks, picnicking, fishing, horseback riding, snowplay-innertube run, cross-country skiing, snowshoeing, snowmobiling, exhibits, av programs; *Facilities:* lodging (National Park Inn & Paradise Inn, 206-475-6260), restaurants, post office; *Services:* first aid, groceries, supplies, gas, equipment rentals, religious services, publications, film.

North Cascades National Park

Mailing address: 800 State St., Sedro Woolley, WA 98284; *Telephone:* 206-855-1331; *Location:* hdqs. in Sedro Woolley; Concrete Information Center, 32 km (20mi) east of Sedro Woolley on Washington 20; entrance to park area 88 km (55 mi) east of Int 55 on Washington 20; *Fees:* camping $3; *Activities:* camping, hiking, self-guiding trails, backcountry use, interpretive talks/walks, picnicking, fishing, mountain climbing, boating, exhibits, av programs; *Facilities:* lodging (North Cascades Lodge, 509-662-3822, Stehekin), restaurant; *Services:* first aid, groceries, supplies, gas, boat rentals, religious services, publications, film.

Olympic National Park

Mailing address: 600 East Park Ave., Port Angeles, WA 98362; *Telephone:* 206-452-4501; *Location:* headquarters at Port Angeles; *Fees:* camping $3; *Activities:* camping, hiking, backcountry use, interpretive talks/walks, picnicking, fishing, swimming, horseback riding, biking, downhill/cross-country skiing, boating, exhibits, av programs; *Facilities:* lodging (Kalaloch Beach Ocean Village, 206-962-2271; Log Cabin Resort, 206-928-3245; Lake Crescent Lodge, 206-928-3211; Sol Duc Hot Springs, 206-928-3211), restaurants; *Services:* first aid, groceries, supplies, gas, equipment rentals, religious services, publications, film.

Petrified Forest National Park

Mailing address: Petrified Forest National Park, AZ 86028; *Telephone:* 602-524-6228; *Location:* 42 km (26 mi) east of Holbrook on Int 40; *Fees:* entrance $1; *Activities:* camping, hiking, self-guiding trails, backcountry use, interpretive talks/walks, picnicking, exhibits, av programs; *Facilities:* none; *Services:* first aid, food, gas, publications, film.

Redwood National Park

Mailing address: Estes Park, CO 80517; *Telephone:* 303-586-2371; *Telephone:* 707-464-6101; *Location:* off US 101 north and south, US 199 from east; *Fees:* none; *Activities:* hiking, self-guiding trails, backcountry use, interpretive talks/walks, picnicking, fishing, swimming, boating, beachcombing (activities in nearby state parks); *Facilities:* none; *Services:* first aid, religious services, publications.

Rocky Mountain National Park

Mailing address: Estes Park, CO 80517; *Telephone:* 303-586-2371;

Location: from Denver, west on Int 70, north on US 40 to Granby, US 34 to Grand Lake entrance; north on Int 25 to Longmont, Colorado 66 to US 36 to Estes Park; US 36 through Boulder to Estes Park; *Fees:* entrance $2, camping $4; *Activities:* camping, hiking, self-guiding trails, backcountry use, interpretive talks/ walks, picnicking, fishing, horseback riding, mountain climbing, downhill/cross-country skiing, snowshoeing, exhibits, av programs; *Facilities:* food service; *Services:* first aid, publications, film.

Sequoia and Kings Canyon National Parks

Mailing address: Three Rivers, CA 93271 (both parks are under the same administration); *Telephone:* 209-565-3341; *Location:* Sequoia on California 198 east from US 99; Kings Canyon on California 180 east of US 99; Generals Highway connects California 198 & 180 through Sequoia to Kings Canyon; *Fees:* entrance $2, camping $2; *Activities:* camping, hiking, self-guiding trails, backcountry use, interpretive talks/walks, picnicking, fishing, horseback riding, downhill/cross-country skiing, exhibits, av programs; *Facilities:* lodging (Sequoia – Sequoia and Kings Canyon Hospitality Service, 209-565-3373; Kings Canyon – Wilsonia Lodge, 209-335-2310), restaurants, post office; *Services:* first aid, supplies, equipment rentals, publications, film.

Shenandoah National Park

Mailing address: Luray, VA 22835; *Telephone:* 703-999-2243: *Location:* 6.4 km (4 mi) west of Thornton Gap & 6.4 km (4 mi) east of Luray on US 211; *Fees:* entrance $2, camping $3; *Activities:* camping, hiking, self-guiding trails, backcountry use, interpretive talks/walks, picnicking, fishing, horseback riding, biking; *Facilities:* lodging (Big Meadow Lodge, Skyland Lodge, 703-743-5108), restaurants; *Services:* first aid, groceries, supplies, gas, publications, film.

Theodore Roosevelt National Park

Mailing address: Medora, ND 58645; *Telephone:* 701-623-4466; *Location:* North Unit, 24 km (15 mi) south of Watford City, 88.5 km (55 mi) north of Belfield on US 85; South Unit, at Medora, 27 km (17 mi) west of Belfield, 101 km (63 mi) east of Glendive, off Int 94, US 10; *Fees:* entrance $2, camping $2; *Activities:* camping, hiking, self-guiding trails, backcountry use, interpretive talks/walks, picnicking, fishing, canoeing, cross-country skiing, exhibits, av programs; *Facilities:* none; *Services:* first aid, publications.

Virgin Islands National Park

Mailing address: P.O. Box 806, Charlotte Amalie, St. Thomas, VI 00801; *Telephone:* 809-776-6201; *Location:* charter or private boat, 8.9 km (5.5 mi) sail from Christiansted; *Fees:* none; *Activities:* hiking, interpretive talks/walks, picnicking, fishing, swimming, snorkeling, exhibits, av programs; *Facilities:* none; *Services:* first aid, publications, film.

Voyageurs National Park

Mailing address: P.O. Box 50, International Falls, MN 56649; *Telephone:* 218-283-9821; *Location:* from Duluth, to Black Bay Narrows entrance via US 53, 280 km (175 mi); to Lake Kabetogama entrance via US 53 & county 122, 240 km (150 mi); to Ash River entrance via US 53 & county 129, 240 km (150 mi); to Crane Lake entrance via US 53 & county 23-24, 240 km (150 mi); *Fees:* none; *Activities:* accessible by boat only – camping, hiking, backcountry use, fishing, swimming, picnicking, interpretive talks/walks, cross-country skiing, snowmobiling, exhibits, av programs; *Facilities:* lodging (Kettle Falls Motel, 218-374-3511; Whispering Pines Resort, 218-374-3321), restaurants; *Services:* first aid, groceries, boat supplies, boat gas, minor boat repairs, equipment rentals, publications, film.

Wind Cave National Park

Mailing address: Hot Springs, SD 57747; *Telephone:* 605-745-4600; on US 385, 17.7 km (11 mi) north of Hot Springs; *Fees:* camping $3; *Activities:* camping, hiking, guided cave tours, interpretive talks/walks, picnicking, exhibits, av programs; *Facilities:* cafeteria; *Services:* first aid, publications, film.

Yellowstone National Park

Mailing address: Yellowstone National Park, WY 82190; *Telephone:* 307-344-7381; *Location:* on US 89, 212, 20, 14, 16, 26, 191 & 287; *Fees:* entrance $2, camping $3; *Activities:* camping, hiking, self-guiding trails, backcountry use, interpretive talks/walks, picnicking, fishing, horseback riding, cross-country skiing, snowshoeing, snowmobiling, exhibits, av programs; *Facilities:* lodging (several lodges, Yellowstone Division, TWA Services, Inc., 307-344-7311), restaurants, post office; *Services:* first aid, groceries, supplies, gas, minor auto repairs, equipment (boat) rentals, religious services, publications, film.

Yosemite National Park

Mailing address: P.O. Box 577, Yosemite National Park, CA 95389; *Telephone:* 209-372-4605; *Location:* California 140 & 120, east from Merced and Manteca; California 41, north from Fresno; California 120, west from Lee Vining (closed in winter); *Fees:* entrance $3, camping $4; *Activities:* camping, hiking, self-guiding trails, backcountry use, interpretive talks/walks, fishing, swimming, horseback riding, mountain climbing, picnicking, downhill/cross-country skiing, exhibits, av programs; *Facilities:* lodging (Yosemite Park and Curry Co., 209-373-4171), restaurants; *Services:* first aid, groceries, supplies, gas, minor auto repairs, equipment rentals, laundry, religious services, publications, film.

Zion National Park

Mailing address: Springdale, UT 84767; *Telephone:* 801-772-3256; *Location:* on Utah 9, 45 km (28 mi) east of Int 15, 40 km (25 mi) west of US 89; *Fees:* entrance $2, camping $2; *Activities:* camping, hiking, self-guiding trails, backcountry use, interpretive talks/ walks, mountain climbing, picnicking, horseback riding, exhibits, av programs; *Facilities:* lodging (Zion Lodge, 800-634-6951), restaurant, post office; *Services:* first aid, religious services, publications, film.

ACKNOWLEDGMENTS

The author is grateful to the following publishers for permission to reprint excerpts from selected material as noted below.

Appalachian Wilderness, Eliot Porter, 1975, E. P. Dutton
The Challenge of Rainier, Dee Molenaar, 1971, The Mountaineers
Hawaii, James A. Michener, 1959, Random House, Inc.
The Longest Cave, Roger W. Brucker and Richard A. Watson, 1976, Alfred A. Knopf, Inc.
My Wilderness: The Pacific West, William O. Douglas, 1960, Doubleday and Company

The National Parks, Michael Frome, 1979, Rand McNally
The National Parks, Freeman Tilden, 1976, Alfred A. Knopf, Inc.
The National Parks of America, Stewart L. Udall, 1966, Country Beautiful Corporation
Reflections From the North Country, Sigurd Olson, 1976, Alfred A. Knopf, Inc.
The Sound of Mountain Water, Wallace Stegner, 1969, Doubleday and Company

National Geographic Magazine, July 1964, "Finding the Mt. Everest of all Living Things," Paul A. Zahl, Ph.D.
